# A
# BITTERN
# CRY

Mollie Carter & Francis Ledwidge, Basingstoke, May 1915
(*Alice Curtayne Collection, Meath County Archive*)

# A BITTERN CRY

in honour of

## FRANCIS LEDWIDGE

Edited by
**TOM FRENCH**

With an introduction by
**GERALD DAWE**

MEATH COUNTY COUNCIL
THE FRANCIS LEDWIDGE MUSEUM &
POETRY IRELAND / ÉIGSE ÉIREANN

*A Bittern Cry* is first published
in a hardback edition
on 31 July 2017
by The Francis Ledwidge Museum,
Poetry Ireland / Éigse Éireann & Meath County Council

ISBN 978 1 900923 309

A CIP catalogue record for this book
is available from the British Library.

Book design & layout by Niall McCormack
Set in Espinosa Nova and Zilvertype Pro

# CONTENTS

*If one who looked from a tower for a new star,*

*watching for years the same part of the sky,*

*suddenly saw it (quite by chance*

*while thinking of other things), and knew it*

*for the star for which he had hoped,*

*how many millions of men would never care?*

*And the star might blaze over the deserts*

*and forests and seas, cheering lost wanderers*

*in desolate lands, or guiding dangerous quests;*

*millions would never know it.*

*And a poet is no more than a star.*

excerpt from Dunsany's introduction
to *Songs of the Fields* (1916)

*see
Complete
Poems
of Ledwidge*

# EDITOR'S NOTE

*... Earth voices ...*

*Earth voices in the branches,*
*butterflies at the flowers*
*on overgrown trenches,*
*and recent graves, replace*
*the historical nightmares.*
*Now we can die in peace.*

**DEREK MAHON**
from *A Quiet Cottage*
(The Gallery Press, 2009)

A BEAUTIFUL sentence in Anne Michaels' *Fugitive Pieces*, regarding the dead, reads, 'It seems right to keep bringing them something beautiful now and then.' In the case of those killed in war, that sentiment seems more true; and, in the case of poets killed in war, more true again.

The contributors to this volume – contacted by Twitter, Facebook and electronic mail – were asked to contribute to an idea that had a title but no shape. The only clear thought was that it should begin and end with Dunsany. The impulse was simply *to do something* for Ledwidge. The writers would be given their heads.

*... poets killed in war ...*

The responses – from Manchester, Florida, Dublin, Aberdeenshire, California, Navan, Belfast, the Irish midlands – were prompt, and they said different things. Some mentioned things they had written previously which, they felt, should be 'left to oblivion.' Others wrote – 'There are poems of his that I love'; 'I will see what I can unearth'; 'It's good to hear his centenary is being marked'; '[He] is an important figure.'

Everything they said boiled down to 'yes'. The only questions were about the number of words and when they would be needed.

Among the contributors are combatants drawn to the subject of home, non-combatants drawn to the subject of war, poets and writers who have dedicated their lives to the craft of discovering order and beauty in words.

Gathered here are the beautiful things writers of different generations bring to Francis Ledwidge in the centenary of his death. In these pages they break bread with one of their own whose fate, to borrow Sebastian Barry's beautiful phrase, 'was written in a ferocious chapter of the book of life'.

Navan, May 2017

# INTRODUCTION

## Gerald Dawe

*I follow on through dangerous zones,*
*Cross dead men's bones and oceans stormy*

**FRANCIS LEDWIDGE**
'The Lanawn Shee'

# I

**IN THE** summer of 2016 myself and a friend walked up Church Street in downtown Enniskillen in search of my maternal grandparents' business and home. We found it after a short spell at the top of the road. This was where my grandfather's mother's people had come from; long before there were borderlands. I knew very little about this side of the family so in a promise to my late mother I was on a bit of a quest. It turned out that the Bradshaws and the Darraghs had connected well and produced a lively young family, including Norman, a small dapper man, who I met once in 1961 when he visited our house after the death of his wife, Ethel, my grandmother. That marriage hadn't worked out so his being back in Belfast – he had happily remarried in England – was a bit of an event. He struck me as a wonderful man, with a slight style of a soldier about him, but I thought no more of it until that day last summer. The rain started to increase so we retreated to my friend's house in the country and continued the pursuit of Norman online. With the instinct and smarts of my friend's son, it was only a matter of minutes before he had established that Norman had in fact joined up as little more than a boy to the Royal Inniskilling Fusiliers; something my mother certainly did not know. I can't say whether he saw military service but the bizarre thing is that when it came to my own mother's time, she married a touring soldier from the Inniskillings, a non-combatant, a musician in the Army band.

Behind this coincidence lies another involving the house where both grandmother and mother lived for a period of time during the 1920s to the 1940s. It was in Duncairn Gardens in north Belfast. The house no longer stands. It was demolished sometime in the late 1970s or early 1980s. While I was never in that house I knew it well. It featured greatly in my mother's retellings of her life growing up there and one of the bus routes I took with my pals going into Belfast city centre passed by the house. We also used to walk along the Antrim Road nearby. I was aware that this had once been my mother's house and that it had a symbolic value in the family's sense of itself.

A tall, three-storied, double-fronted Victorian house with a small garden in front and a backyard; during the early decades it had witnessed the growing-up of two children, my mother and her brother, evening soirées, organised by their mother, refugees passing through during the 1930s and the Blitz of 1941. My mother recalled lances that had been used to hold drapes in place in the upper front room and the violin playing of a refugee family who her mother had befriended; the calling to the house of an itinerant street-seller utterly taken aback when the woman of the house, Mary Jane Quartz spoke to him in Gujarati from her time spent in India with her temperamental Regimental sergeant-major of a father.

The house number, 163, was a number that bore a kind of secretive vibrancy in my boyhood. But what I could not expect was how that private personal story would intersect with the tragedy of Francis Ledwidge. For it was in that house, if I have read the records correctly, that Robert Christie lived and, if that is the case, this would have been the house that his good friend Francis Ledwidge visited on his delayed return to Ebrington Barracks and the troubled encounter with his superiors in Derry prior to the fateful embarkation to France in 1917. It would seem that the Inniskillings had played a role in my family's past without a shot being fired or a battle fought. I can only assume that my great grandfather had bought the house from the Christie family some time in the 1920s. It was sold shortly after his death in the late 1940s.

## II

I retell this story for a simple reason, but one which is often overlooked, even to this day, when the realities of our community past is opening up in a way unimaginable twenty or thirty years ago. The experience of war and the variable, coincidental lives of hundreds of thousands of Irish men and women are inextricably linked *across* the island of Ireland, north, south, east and west. The British Army provided, whether we like it or not, an economic, social and, by now, historical link that runs deep within our society. Francis Ledwidge is an expression of this, as the contradictions explored throughout this powerful collection of essays, poems and reflections makes plain.

Ledwidge embodies the central dynamic forces at play in Irish society in the early decades of the last century; at so many levels his personal and cultural story contrasts with and challenges the dominant narratives of nationalism and unionism. As *A Bittern*

*Cry* demonstrates, Ledwidge's attractiveness to poets and writers from his own time to the present has produced (quite literally in Seán Dunne's essay and poem) a sense of pilgrimage in much of the work that follows.

It were as if Ledwidge represents, in his life story but also in his ambition, effort, and fate, a different kind of bearing on what happened to and in Ireland during and since the First World War. Ledwidge is our imaginative way through the mire of history. He is our guide to what became of this society, wracked by violent and prolonged struggle for independence, the civil war which followed and the short-sighted partition with its tragic and deep-seated consequences for both sides of the border. Ledwidge is a harbinger of what damage would be done in the subsequent decades with the loss of what could well have turned out to be a powerful poetic voice – but also the silencing of his complicating presence to generations of young Irish students and readers of poetry. Ledwidge's love of countryside and knowledge of, in particular, his beloved Meath are, as we discover in many of these engaging portraits, matched by his exposure to other places – Dublin, Belfast, Derry, Manchester, Turkey, Serbia, Egypt. His developing reputation in London, his appetite for reading, learning more, and his self-awareness of what he wanted to achieve as a poet suggests a steely resolve in the dire circumstances of war, not unlike that of Wilfred Owen's.

However, while Owen, or Isaac Rosenberg, produced a new kind of poetic language over their short life-spans, Ledwidge's language in most of his writing remained close to the conventions of a popular pastoral mode much enjoyed and respected by readers and reciters of poetry. His association with the Georgian 'movement' is significant though and places Ledwidge as a poet at the critical bridgehead between nineteenth and twentieth century and the 'breakthrough' into a different kind of poetic, something we hear in the hypnotic poetry of Edward Thomas. Ledwidge was known by his fellow poets in Ireland and Britain but crucially he was also identified by Siegfried Sassoon, among others, as a presence within the world of war poetry. Where this might have led him, like Edmund Blunden for instance, *post-war*, is one of those unanswerable questions.

As the peerless Con Houlihan remarks in his adeptly comparative essay, Ledwidge's mother 'was free from the worst of all Irish diseases – self-pity', so too Francis resisted self-serving notions of Irishness. Might one assume that had he survived the war he would have, like Thomas MacGreevy, sought out different ways of expressing himself in new poetic subjects; or like Patrick McGill, turned perhaps to prose; certainly his letters (deserving a critical edition all to themselves) suggest as much as a possibility.

Ledwidge's rich aural imagination, the musical line and unforced ease with the rhythms of ordinary speech, demonstrates time and again the verbal skills he had at his disposal; a perfect 'ear' for the sound of how English is spoken in rural Ireland. Whether he could have aligned all this with more demanding, problematic subject-matter does not really bear thinking about, given his tragic loss at such a young age.

*A Bittern Cry* makes a lasting and just testament to Francis Ledwidge the man and poet and to the culture out of which he came; a timely honour indeed from his very heartland of Meath. Edited with great care by Tom French and published by the pioneering Francis Ledwidge Museum, Slane in association with Meath County Library Service and Poetry Ireland, this anthology marks a crucial landmark in the growing visibility of a once critically forgotten voice. Hopefully, in due course we will see Ledwidge's life and work and the contexts of both receive the kind of scholarly attention similar to recent studies of, for example,

Isaac Rosenberg or David Jones. On the road ahead, however, this necessary book will be a lighthouse beacon showing the way. Ledwidge is a representative figure, illuminating the past certainly, but in his courage, contradictions and personality, he reveals a truer, more human vision of ourselves; on this ground alone *A Bittern Cry* deserves a wide and lasting readership.

Dún Laoghaire,
Easter Monday 2017

# THE AUNT'S STORY    ❦    *Gerald Dawe*


The first time in London, a family wedding.
I had my new school uniform on
and Great Uncle Bill stood in the perfect garden
of his home telling me to spell *character*.

The cats sat blinking in a far-off corner
and Eileen – *she never lost the accent* –
watched her sister's grandson perform.
The sky was bright as could be.

What walked in the shadow was The War,
the long road back, the swish of evening gowns,
as the girls crept in late to the god-awful groan
of their father in his own bedroom;

the half-opened door, and give-away stairs.
Her face at the kitchen window has the look
of someone distracted by what never was.
*C.H.A.R* ...


from *Heart of Hearts*
(The Gallery Press, 1995)

Francis Ledwidge Museum Committee, Janeville 1981 – l to r: Paddy Mongey,
Vivien Igoe, John Clarke, Bobby Doonan, Pearl Baxter, Joe Ledwidge, Peter Baxter
*(courtesy of the Francis Ledwidge Museum)*

# JANEVILLE

*Gareth Yore*

*When you come in, it seems a brighter fire*
*Crackles upon the hearth invitingly,*
*The household routine which was wont to tire*
*Grows full of novelty.*

THESE LINES, from Ledwidge's poem 'To One Who Comes Now and Then', celebrate the company he enjoyed with his close friend Matty McGoona, and describe the scene as Matty enters the kitchen in Janeville, Slane, County Meath.

Janeville and its hearth were in many ways the heart of Ledwidge's poetry, but in recent years it has evolved to more than that. Its renovation as a museum in the 1980s dedicated to the memory of the poet has seen Janeville evolve into a focal point of remembrance and celebration of Ledwidge for both the local community and for a broader national and international audience.

The Ledwidge cottage was described by the poet's biographer Alice Curtayne, in glowing terms:

> *In addition to its attractive freshness, the house was spacious compared with their first home: three bedrooms, large kitchen, living-room, half an acre of ground at the back for a garden. Even today the sturdy little house still occupies an enviable site, elevated, open and salubrious, with a delightful view of Meath across the valley of the Boyne.*

In addition to the joy of Francis's birth in 1887 the family experienced the further joy of the birth of his brother Joseph in 1891. The day-to-day life in Janeville and the fond childhood memories, inextricably linked to his mother, educated the poet and influenced his writing. Reminiscing on his childhood, he wrote fondly of that time:

> *These stories told at my mother's doorstep in the owl's light were the first things I remember, except perhaps the old songs which she sang to me ... so full of romance, love and sacrifice.*

The beauty of Janeville and its environs hides in plain sight in much of Ledwidge's writing. His poem 'June' revels in the beauty of the month with the opening lines linked to the cottage and its garden:

> *Broom out the floor now, lay the fender by,*
> *And plant this bee-sucked bough of woodbine there,*
> *And let the window down. The butterfly*
> *Floats in upon the sunbeam, and the fair*
> *Tanned face of June ...*

Bad and good times followed hot on each other's heels. Tragedy struck in 1892 with the sudden death of Patrick, Francis's father, at the age of only 52. Francis wrote of this in later years:

> *I often asked her of my father (who died when I was four) but was always reproved by her eyes and so I learned to leave that side of her life severely alone.*

Further tragedy befell when the eldest son Patrick returned home from Dublin suffering from tuberculosis. The tragedy was not only his lingering death but also the loss to the family of its main source of income. Francis remembered:

> *My mother laboured night and day as none of us was strong enough to provide for our wants. She never complained and even when my eldest brother advanced in strength she persisted in his regular attendance at school until he qualified at book-keeping and left for Dublin. His position carried a respectable salary.*

The family was on the brink of eviction from Janeville. An eviction notice for rent arrears was served but could not be carried out as Patrick was deemed not fit to be moved. Ledwidge, describing the torment of this time, wrote:

> *Oh those four years. It was as though God forgot us.*

The family survived by the skin of its teeth and Francis grew up in Janeville's 'half an acre of ground at the back for a garden', which offered the poet a ready-made natural observatory. The garden at that time would have been more functional than ornate as the ground provided the family with vegetables. Its wild and organic nature are exactly what appealed to the poet:

> *I hated gardens where gaudy flowers were trained in rows but loved the wild things of change and circumstance.*

The link between the garden, his love of nature and the special love for his mother all combine in his poem 'The Gardener':

> *Among the flowers, like flowers, her slow hands move*
> *Easing a muffled bell or stooping low*
> *To help sweet roses climb the stakes above*
> *Where pansies stare and seem to whisper 'Lo!'*

The lure of Janeville proved very strong for the young poet. At the age of 15 his mother organised for Francis to start work as a grocer's apprentice in Larry Carpenter's grocery in Drogheda. He lodged over the shop because the hours of work of a grocer's apprentice were long. This did not suit the young poet who suffered from homesickness, even though he was allowed home from Saturday afternoon to Sunday evening. Yet, if the seven miles from Drogheda to Slane seemed far to the young poet, the thirty miles to Rathfarnham must have felt like another universe. Francis was to replace his brother Michael (who had been offered a better job) as a grocer's apprentice in Daly's of Rathfarnham. Predictably, the poet 'could not bear the brick horizons' which the city presented and 'all [his] dreams called [him] home'. One fateful night he stole out of the grocer's and walked the thirty miles back to Janeville and his mother. His longing for home while in the city is epitomised in his first poem of note, 'Behind the Closed Eye', which opens with the verse:

> *I walk the old frequented ways*
> *That wind around the tangled braes,*
> *I live again the sunny days*
> *Ere I the city knew*

The poet's checkered employment history contrasts with the constancy of his devotion to his home. At the age of 19, having lost his job as yard boy for the Carlyle family at Newgrange, Ledwidge declared:

> *I determined never to leave home again, so I took up any old job*
> *at all with local farmers and was happy.*

Any old job extended to a stint as a miner in the local copper mine at Beauparc. However, his subterranean adventure did not last long as he attempted to organise a strike for better conditions and was summarily dismissed. He was now 22 and, in need of employment, Ledwidge went to work on the roads for Meath County Council and, after a short period he was promoted to foreman which required his being based some 20 miles away in Kells and the taking of lodgings. The lure of home was as strong as ever and Francis made the journey home almost every Saturday evening.

As the poet matured the pull of home was gradually usurped by his 'wildness for wandering to far-off places'. At the age of 27 the poet left Janeville to enlist and fight in the Great War. The horrors of that war and the outcome of the 1916 Rising in which his friend and fellow poet Thomas MacDonagh was executed by the same army in which Ledwidge served, left the poet disillusioned on his return to Janeville for a period of leave in May 1916. His friends found him changed and morose. He told his brother Joe:

> *If I heard the Germans were coming in over our back wall, I wouldn't go out now to stop them. They could come!*

This was to be his last time at home. In early August 1917 Anne Ledwidge, Francis's mother, opened a letter sent to her from Father Devas which read:

> *Dear Mrs Ledwidge,*
>
> *I do not know how to write to you about the death of your dear son, Francis. Quite apart from his wonderful gifts, he was such a lovable boy and I was so fond of him ... That evening while out with a working party a shell exploded quite near to them killing seven and wounding twelve. Francis was killed at once, so suffered no pain. I like to think that God took him before the world had been able to spoil him with its praise and he has found far greater joy and beauty than ever he would have found on earth ...*

Janeville entered a new phase. The eight surviving Ledwidge children grew into their own lives. Following Anne Ledwidge's death on 9 April 1926 at the age of 72, her daughter Annie came to live in the cottage with her husband John Phelan and they in turn had two sons, Enda and Roland. Local historian and Ledwidge Cottage Museum Committee member Jimmy McComiskey remembers visiting the Phelans in Janeville on many occasions. He recalls walking the round trip of some eight miles from the Pump Cross, Rathdrinagh to Janeville with his grandmother Mrs Cregan. Jimmy was about nine years old at the time, which means the visits occurred circa 1945. He used to be sent out to the garden to play while the adults conversed and he remembers sitting in the wild back garden under the damson tree eating damsons. As a consequence, to this day, Jimmy can't stand the sight of that fruit. He remembers a big table in front of the window, a settle bed and a dresser.

Roland Phelan lived in the cottage until his own death in December 1978. His brother Enda, who had emigrated to England, placed an advertisement in *The Irish Times* in the summer of 1979 which read 'Poet's Cottage for Sale'. The local community realised the opportunity the sale of the cottage represented. The sale was brought to the attention of the Slane Community Council and it was decided to form the Ledwidge Cottage Committee which set the purchase of the cottage as its objective. Fittingly, the first meeting of the committee was held in Crewbawn, a location eulogised in Ledwidge's poem of the same name. The meeting was held on 18 October 1979 in Garda Sergeant John Clarke's house in Crewbawn. The minutes of that first meeting read as follows:

> *A meeting of the Francis Ledwidge House Committee was held in Clarke's of Crewbawn. The following attended – Pearl Baxter, Peter Baxter, John Clarke, Patrick Mongey and Bobby*

*Doonan. Peter Baxter was appointed Chairman and John Clarke, Secretary.*

Rosemary Yore, current chairperson of the committee and daughter of Pearl and Peter Baxter, recalls the time and the drive of the committee members to purchase the cottage. She recalls her mother saying, "We can't let this go. We have to get that cottage."

This drive to purchase the cottage was natural, as the seeds of community remembrance of Ledwidge had been sown some 18 years earlier with the erection of the Ledwidge Memorial Plaque on the bridge in Slane on 9 September 1962. This was an initiative of the Slane Guild of Muintir na Tíre, an organisation founded by Canon John Hayes, which promoted community work and engagement. A bronze plaque was commissioned by the Guild and executed by sculptor Seamus Murphy RHA for the sum of £80. The original plaque which is now on the front wall of the cottage, with a copy also at Slane bridge, quotes lines from the poet's most famous poem, 'Lament for Thomas MacDonagh':

> *He shall not hear the bittern cry*
> *In the wild sky, where he is lain,*
> *Nor voices of the sweeter birds*
> *Above the wailing of the rain*

The commissioning of the plaque was not without its complications. The original version bore '1891' as the poet's birth year instead of the correct date of 1887. The sculptor observed in correspondence that: 'every source gives the date as 1891 but if this is established as incorrect, we have no option but to change it'. The error was corrected but, sadly, Seamus Murphy was too ill to travel to see the unveiling of his finished work.

The unveiling event was a unique gathering from a generation associated with the poet. Attendees included Joseph Ledwidge, brother of the poet and his sons Frank and Joe, Annie Phelan, sister of the poet and her sons Enda and Roland Phelan. Also present were former classmates of the poet in Slane National School - Father Michael Marry, John Ward and William Kerrigan, father of current committee member Tom Kerrigan. They were joined by Alice Curtayne, Stephen Rynne, Frank O'Connor, Donagh MacDonagh, son of Thomas MacDonagh, Winifred McGoona, sister of Matty McGoona, and Lord Dunsany, son of the poet's patron. Interestingly, the record of the event gives special mention to Joe Ledwidge, son of Joseph Ledwidge and his wonderful singing voice.

Some 18 years later the Ledwidge Cottage Committee continued this community initiative and engaged in fundraising to raise the money required to purchase the cottage. The committee received over 140 individual donations ranging from £1 to £5,000, which totalled over £16,000. The list of donors was interesting in itself and included large corporations such as Tara Mines, philanthropic organisations such as the Ireland Fund of America, local people, poets Peter Fallon, Michael Longley and John Hewitt, author of *Strumpet City* James Plunkett, the British Broadcasting Corporation (BBC), Lord and Lady Mountcharles and civil servant *sans pareil* TK Whitaker.

The funds raised in conjunction with a Community Council interest-free loan of £2,000 enabled the committee to purchase the cottage for the sum of £8,000 plus legal costs, in February 1980. The remaining balance of the monies raised was used to undertake the substantial renovation works required. The cottage was restored through the hard work of local volunteers, friends of the Ledwidge cause and workers from AnCO, the precursor to FÁS. The work took approximately a year and, apart from restoring the cottage to its original state, the back garden designed by Phoenix

Park superintendent Dr John A McCullen, was transformed into a heart-shaped space.

An instance of community spirit as part of the restoration project was the moving of the trysting stone from the Hill of Slane to the back garden of the cottage. The trysting stone was said to have been the place where Francis courted Ellie Vaughey and was located effectively in Ellie's family's back garden. The stone itself must weigh about two tonnes, the moving of which represented a significant logistical challenge even in an era of heavy machinery. It was moved the two miles between the Hill and the cottage over three evenings by the men of the committee with the help of machinery from Cement-Roadstone Ltd and their employees Danny Bagnal, Tommy Nevin and Tommy Lenehan. The final stage of its journey saw it transported through Mrs Ethel McKeever's land and it was unloaded over the boundary fence to the corner of the back garden of the cottage where it rests today, accompanied by a stone plaque with the following lines from 'To One Dead':

> A blackbird singing
> I hear in my troubled mind,
> Bluebells swinging
> I see in a distant wind.
> But sorrow and silence
> Are the wood's threnody,
> The silence for you
> And the sorrow for me.

The restored cottage was opened in a ceremony performed by Dr Benedict Kiely on 20 June 1982. As an eight-year-old child I have only vague recollections of the ceremony itself, but a memory that still resonates with me is Dr Kiely's melodious tones echoing for years through the cottage. Dr Kiely kindly agreed to recite a number of Ledwidge poems and a recording was played through speakers in the cottage when visitors arrived. Having worked as a guide in the cottage I knew this tape off by heart and can still hear Dr Kiely's soft Tyrone accent reciting the penultimate verse of 'Behind the Closed Eye' so beautifully that it sounded as if the poet had known the voice and had written the lines specifically for him:

> *And wondrous impudently sweet,*
> *Half of him passion, half conceit,*
> *The blackbird calls adown the street*
> *Like the piper of Hamelin*

Dr Kiely's address was received by an audience which included the poet's three nephews Joe and Frank Ledwidge and Roland Phelan, actor Cyril Cusack, writer James Plunkett, Lord Dunsany, son of the poet's patron, and Winnie McGoona, sister of Matty. The opening ceremony marked the next phase of the cottage's existence and opened the poet's home to patrons from far and near. On his visit on 26 August 1990 President Patrick J Hillery planted a cherry tree in the back garden. The President's visit was celebrated with a large gathering in the cottage garden as described in the committee minutes by committee secretary, Pearl Baxter:

> *The day dawned warm and cloudy with intermittent burst of*
> *sunshine and the cottage never looked more lovely. The village*
> *was dressed in its Sunday best ... There was a plaque to unveil in*
> *the cottage to commemorate his visit which he duly did and paid*
> *tribute to its beauty ... the weather took a hand to spoiling the*
> *closing stages by sending a heavy summer shower just as the tree*
> *was being planted, so at least we know that it got a good start.*
> *Previous to that the sun was delightful and the whole garden*
> *scene was idyllic with soft warm air filled with soothing music*
> *and the huge gathering revelled in the glorious occasion.*

In his address the President paid tribute to both the poet and the committee. On receiving gifts of *A Life of the Poet* and his *Complete Poems*, Dr Hillery commented:

> *I shall assure you that I will read these wonderful books and read and re-read them. I'll absolutely cherish them ... What you have done in the opening of the Francis Ledwidge Cottage Museum is worthy of the highest acclaim and congratulations. You are paying tribute to genius and keeping green the memory of a poet whose loss was irreparable.*

Among the other distinguished guests who have visited the cottage over the years, I remember the impromptu private visit of then Taoiseach, Charles J Haughey in July 1991. It happened that Mr Haughey was passing through Slane *en route* to another event and agreed to visit the cottage on his way. As a child what I remember clearly is not the admiration in which others held their political idol, but the fact that he produced a brand new £50 note from his pocket as a donation to the cottage. I had never seen its like before and it looked almost exotic to young eyes and was presented by its owner in the way a magician might conjure a rabbit from a hat.

Another visit of note was that of Mrs Jean Kennedy Smith in August 1993. Mrs Smith, sister of JF Kennedy, was at that time the American Ambassador to Ireland and paid her visit on her way to Newgrange. In 2015 the cottage received an impromptu visit from 007, aka Pierce Brosnan. Mr. Brosnan arrived unannounced and decided to stop off on his way to another engagement. The incognito nature of the Navan-born actor's visit, in keeping with his most famous character, was for the cottage guide Ann McGivern's eyes only, as she was the only person there at the time.

One of the most fruitful visits to the cottage was that of Seamus Heaney in 1984. It marked the beginning of a relationship which was to greatly enhance Ledwidge's international profile. Following the visit in 1984 the Committee kept in touch with Mr Heaney and invited him to become a member of the 1987 committee which commemorated the centenary of the poet's birth in 1887. Mr Heaney replied to the invitation in a letter dated 12 February 1987:

> *Your letter arrived here on the day of your first committee meeting so I regret I was not in touch with you in time to let you know that I would be happy to join the Ledwidge Centenary Committee.*

Unsurprisingly, the poet goes on to outline in the correspondence that he had various engagements planned for that year and says:

> *In other words, I don't foresee that I am going to be a very useful or active addition to your team.*

However, Seamus Heaney's contribution to the committee exceeded that description of 'very useful'. In further correspondence, dated 4 August 1987, Mr Heaney states:

> *Thanks for the invitation to the Ledwidge Centenary celebrations. I regret that I cannot join because I go with my family on Thursday week to Cambridge, Massachusetts, to teach for the next year at Harvard.*
>
> *However, I would like to mark the occasion by donating to the Ledwidge Cottage Museum a couple of the worksheets of the poem 'In Memoriam Francis Ledwidge' which appeared in 'Field Work' in 1979. The poem itself was written in 1977, so just missed the centenary by a decade!*

Seamus Heaney remained a true friend of the committee's to the end of his life. The donated worksheets are prominently displayed in the cottage, alongside the finished version of his wonderful 'In Memoriam Francis Ledwidge', the final quatrain of which reads:

> *You followed from Boyne water to the Balkans*
> *But miss the twilit note your flute should sound.*
> *You were not keyed or pitched like these true-blue ones*
> *Though all of you consort now underground.*

The community spirit associated with the Ledwidge Cottage Committee and, by extension, the Janeville project, has always been its strength. It has enabled a local committee to restore and maintain the birthplace and home of the poet and has helped to spread the poetry of Francis Ledwidge to a national and international audience. This spirit is epitomised in the annual Ledwidge Day event held close to the anniversary of the poet's death on 31 July. The typical format of the event took the form of a celebration in the cottage garden during the day and an evening talk by a key speaker in the local hotel.

The entire event, including the erecting of the stage, provision of electrics and acoustics, posters, press and stewarding was organised the committee. The event ran in this format for many years and included notable speakers such as: Anthony Cronin, Ulick O'Connor, Peter Fallon, Keith Jeffery, Ciarán Mac Mathúna, Vivien Igoe, Eamonn Keane, Augustine Martin, Mary Lavin, Vincent Dowling, Desmond Egan, Helen Cooney, Gerald Dawe, Michael Hartnett and Andrew Rynne.

The committee has been blessed with such wonderful speakers over the years who, each in their own way, has presented different angles and interpretations of Ledwidge and his writings. This variety has in turn contributed to the Ledwidge discourse which is a primary aim of the committee. It would be unfair to single out one speaker but it is also impossible to ignore the contributions of such speakers as Michael Hartnett. Michael was known to be a great admirer of Ledwidge and was a great friend of the committee. The speech he delivered in 1992 was noteworthy for its passion as much as for its content. Michael's display of appreciation for the poet was such that it was impossible not to be intoxicated by it. His throwing his jacket onto the floor mid-speech, not pausing for thought, was not a gesture designed for effect; in fact, quite the contrary. His jacket was an impediment to conveying his passion and appreciation of the poet to his audience and, as a consequence, had to be removed.

Mr Andrew Rynne, son of Ledwidge's biographer Alice Curtayne, in his speech titled *My Mother and Francis*, explained to his audience that Ledwidge had not initially been a natural subject of choice for his mother, as she usually wrote about religious figures. He explained that the project came to life on the suggestion of HE John Cardinal Wright who described the cult of Ledwidge in Boston College, Massachusetts. Alice Curtayne was spurred to dedicate eight years of her life to the writing of the biography. Andrew complimented his talk with a stuffed yellow bittern in a glass case which provoked equal measures of interest and amusement among the audience.

Transporting the bittern to the event proved to be an event in itself. Mr Rynne had travelled from Prosperous in Kildare to the Conyngham Arms Hotel with the bittern in the back seat of his car. He nervously entrusted responsibility for the precious cargo to my father to transport to the venue in Slane Castle. While my father, in his profession as a taxi driver, had transported many dubious characters in the back seat of his car over the years, there had never been any more unusual or precious as that thirsty bird. Nothing untoward occurred and the bittern managed to avoid extinction for a second time.

Sadly, the garden event became logistically impossible to continue due to parking restrictions, health and safety requirements and unpredictable weather. Also, as with any amateur organisation, the Ledwidge Day events were not without their opportunities for advancements of learning, which is evident in the secretary's AGM report for 1990:

> *The main event of the year was Ledwidge Day which was an enjoyable occasion with a few hiccups thrown in. The entertainment was much below former years in quality. However, we have learned our lesson and we shan't repeat the mistake.*

While the garden event has had its day the committee has evolved over the years in promoting the writings of Ledwidge to a more international audience. Again Janeville has been at the heart of this which is illustrated in the collaboration of our Belgian colleagues in the erection of the Ledwidge memorial in Boezinghe, near Ieper (Ypres) in Belgium on 31 July 1998, and its identical twin in the garden at Janeville on 29 July 2001.

The son of a former comrade of Francis Ledwidge had written the entire Ledwidge poem 'Crochnaharna' in the visitors' book of Artillery Wood Cemetery where the poet is buried. This brought the poet to the attention of Piet Chielens, director of the In Flanders Fields Museum. As a result, a memorial to commemorate Ledwidge was designed and commissioned by the In Flanders Fields Museum and the city of Ieper.

The monument was erected in Boezinghe in a potato field surrounded by cattle to mark the place where the poet fell 81 years previous to that day. It was constructed from yellow brick with a portrait of the poet etched in glass to give a ghost-like effect. It bears the first two lines of 'Lament for Thomas MacDonagh' and the complete poem 'Soliloquy' in both English and Flemish. The monument was the initiative of the city of Ieper and, to this day, the people of Ieper and Slane enjoy a partnership in remembering Ledwidge. Those in attendance at the day were the Mayor of Ieper Luc Dehane, director of In Flanders Fields Museum, Mr Piet Chielens, secretary of the Irish Embassy Maurice Bigger, poet and writer Dermot Bolger and our very own Joe and Phyllis Ledwidge. Joe paid a moving tribute to his uncle on that day and presented the following lines written, as he said himself, "in rhyme rather than verse".

> *You were born beside Boyne waters*
> *Where the rushes sway and nod*
> *You played and danced and sang your songs*
> *And ploughed Meath's fertile sod.*
>
> *Then you wandered Flanders Fields,*
> *Torn and loud with war,*
> *Far from Boyne and dreamy noon,*
> *With death you were accounted for.*
>
> *In Flanders Fields now warm and kind*
> *War brings no more decay*
> *So from our hearts with pride and joy*
> *We honour you today.*

The replica monument was built in the garden at Janeville by Conrad de Muelenaere and Jean Luc Tillie in the spring of 2001. The Ieper brick and glass panels were sent from the In Flanders Fields Museum in Ieper and Jean Luc and Conrad came over to build them in Flemish bond style. The monument was unveiled on 29 July 2001 by Joe Ledwidge and Pearl Baxter. A contingent travelled from Belgium for the unveiling, including Piet Chielens, Director of In Flanders Fields Museum, Jonny and Rita Claus and Fernand

Vanrobaeys from Ieper Tourist Office. Major Jack Dunlop and his wife represented the Inniskilling Fusiliers Museum, Northern Ireland, and Dermot Bolger was also present. A series of glass panels depicting the poet's life, from his birth in the cottage to his death at the Third Battle of Ypres, were designed by conservation architect Turlough McKevitt and unveiled on the same day.

Three years later the committee was back in Belgium, this time represented by myself, for President McAleese's visit to Ledwidge's grave on 9 June 2004. The auspicious day remains clear in my memory, not least because the President displayed a deep and genuine interest in the poet. It was evident in speaking to her that she knew much about the poet's life and she expressed a deep admiration for his poetry. She also expressed sadness at his loss so young and linked this to the tragedy of the Great War. Her main engagement on this trip to Belgium was a visit to the Irish Peace Park at Messines where she unveiled a plaque bearing Ledwidge's poem 'Soliloquy'.

Other international projects include the collaboration with the Imperial War Museum, London, which saw the launch by Baroness Blackstone, then British Minister for Arts, of the publication *Anthem for Doomed Youth* on 29 October 2002. The book, edited by the late Jon Stallworthy, Professor of English Literature at Oxford, featured twelve poets who fought in the Great War, including Ledwidge.

This was a hugely positive initiative for the promotion of Ledwidge's work. The irony, however, was that Ledwidge's poetry would be promoted in British schools, as the book was to be used to educate children about the First World War, yet his voice remained virtually silent in the Irish education system.

After many years of lobbying the committee was informed in 2013 by the National Council for Curriculum Assessment (NCCA) that Ledwidge was to come back onto the curriculum for the 2015–2018 cycle, but disappointingly this was only for the year 2016 and included only his 'Lament for Thomas MacDonagh'. The inclusion of his most celebrated poem on the 2016 curriculum was contextually appropriate given that it was the centenary of the 1916 rising, but it is nowhere near sufficient if Ledwidge's poetry is to enter the national consciousness of a new generation.

Another fruitful collaboration for the committee has been with the Snowdonia National Park Authority in Wales, which as part of its remit honours the memory and maintains the birthplace of Welsh poet Hedd Wyn (Ellis Humphrey Evans). Hedd Wyn was from a farming background and enlisted with the Royal Welch Fusiliers to save his younger brother Robert from having to enlist. He was killed on the same day as Francis Ledwidge, was the same age and is buried just two rows behind him in Artillery Wood Cemetery, Belgium. In April 2014 Naomi Jones and her colleagues, accompanied by poet Myrddin ap Dafydd visited the cottage. They were welcomed to the cottage by guides Paul Mongey and Catherine Moore, Tom French and committee members Colm and Rosemary Yore. Friendships have been forged and, fittingly, both Francis Ledwidge and Hedd Wyn will be commemorated in Artillery Wood Cemetery on 31 July 2017.

The Janeville story not only encompasses the life and memory of Ledwidge, but also the lives and memories of the local people who have worked to preserve the poet's birthplace and memory through their voluntary work. Their endeavour is motivated by respect and admiration for the poet, pride of place and the pride of family. I am the third generation of my family to be involved in the Ledwidge project, following my grandparents Pearl and Peter Baxter and parents Colm and Rosemary Yore. Committee member Rachel O'Malley continues the work of her father John

Clarke. Helen Tully carries on the work of her father Noel and uncle Raymond Tully. Tom Kerrigan has served on the committee for many years and, in his involvement, honours his father Willie's friendship with the poet. Tom's son Darragh also contributes to the work of the committee through his artistic talent and, seventy years on, Jimmy McComiskey still honours the memory of Ledwidge through his contribution to the committee, (even if he can't go near the damson tree that still stands in the garden). There are also many others, too numerous to mention, both past and present, who, through their voluntary work, continue to maintain Janeville and to love and promote Ledwidge's poetry.

And what of Janeville now and in the future? The committee hopes for 'a brighter fire that crackles upon the hearth invitingly'. There are plans afoot to develop the adjoining cottage, to provide a new vehicle entrance and car park to accommodate coaches, and to redevelop the existing car park into a civic space.

Such ambition is not without its challenges. The Ledwidge story is now being heard by a growing international audience, and the work cannot continue to be done by a local committee. National input and support are needed. Recent collaboration with Meath County Council for the centenary commemoration has greatly facilitated the work of keeping the poet's memory alive and demonstrates what can be achieved. Partnerships of this nature in the future will ensure that Janeville can enter brightly its next phase.

# AN BONNÁN BUÍ ❦ *Cathal Buí Mac Giolla Ghunna*

A bhonnáin bhuí, is é mo chrá do luí
    is do chnámha críon tar éis a gcreim,
is chan díobháil bídh ach easpa dí
    d'fhág tú 'do luí ar chúl do chinn;
is measa liom féin ná scrios na Traí
    thú bheith sínte ar leacaibh lom,
is nach ndearna tú díth ná dolaidh is tír
    is nárbh fhearr leat fíon ná uisce poill.

Is a bhonnáin álainn, mo mhíle crá
    do chúl ar lár amuigh insa tslí,
is gur moch gach lá a chluininn do ghráig
    ar an láib agus tú ag ól na dí;
is é an ní adeir cách le do dheartháir Cathal
    go bhfaighidh mé bás mar súd, más fíor;
ní hamhlaidh atá – súd an préachán breá
    chuaigh a dh'éag ar ball, gan aon bhraon dí.

A bhonnáin óig, is é mo mhíle brón
    thú bheith romham i measc na dtom,
is na lucha móra ag triall chun do thórraimh
    ag déanamh spóirt is pléisiúir ann;
dá gcuirfeá scéala in am fá mo dhéinse
    go raibh tú i ngéibheann nó i mbroid fá dheoch,
do bhrisfinn béim ar an loch sin Vesey
    a fhliuchfadh do bhéal is do chorp isteach.

Ní hé bhur n-éanlaith atá mise ag éagnach,
    an lon, an smaolach, ná an chorr ghlas –
ach mo bhonnán buí a bhí lán den chroí,
    is gur cosúil liom féin é ina ghné is a dhath;
bhíodh sé choíche ag síoról na dí,
    agus deir na daoine go mbím mar sin seal,
is níl deor dá bhfaighead nach ligfead síos
    ar eagla go bhfaighinnse bás den tart.

Dúirt mo stór liom ligean den ól
    nó nach mbeinnse beo ach seal beag gearr,
ach dúirt mé léi go dtug sí bréag
    is gurbh fhaide mo shaolsa an deoch úd a fháil;
nach bhfaca sibh éan an phíobáin réidh
    a chuaigh a dh'éag den tart ar ball? –
a chomharsain chléibh, fliuchaidh bhur mbéal,
    óir chan fhaigheann sibh braon i ndiaidh bhur mbáis.

## THE YELLOW BITTERN ✠ *Thomas MacDonagh*

The yellow bittern that never broke out
    in a drinking bout, might as well have drunk;
his bones are thrown on a naked stone
    where he lived alone like a hermit monk.
O yellow bittern! I pity your lot,
    though they say that a sot like myself is curst –
I was sober a while, but I'll drink and be wise
    for fear I should die in the end of thirst.

It's not for the common birds that I'd mourn,
    the blackbird, the corncrake, or the crane,
but for the bittern that's shy and apart
    and drinks in the marsh from the lone bog-drain.
Oh! If I had known you were near your death,
    while my breath held out I'd have run to you,
till a splash from the Lake of the Son of the Bird
    your soul would have stirred and waked anew.

My darling told me to drink no more
    or my life would be o'er in a little short while;
but I told her 'tis drink gives me health and strength
    and will lengthen my road by many a mile.
You see how the bird of the long smooth neck
    could get his death from the thirst at last –
come, son of my soul, and drain your cup,
    you'll get no sup when your life is past.

In a wintering island by Constantine's halls
        a bittern calls from a wineless place,
and tells me that hither he cannot come
        till the summer is here and the sunny days.
When he crosses the stream there and wings o'er the sea
        then a fear comes to me he may fail in his flight –
well, the milk and the ale are drunk every drop,
        and a dram won't stop our thirst this night.


from the Irish of Cathal Buí Mac Giolla Ghunna

# A PEER FINDS A POET.

Lord Dunsany has discovered a new Irish poet, Mr. Francis Ledwidge, who lives with his mother and brother (seen in the picture) in a cottage at Navan, Co. Meath. The poet has a book in his hand. Lord Dunsany pointed out that Mr. Ledwidge, who is only 22 years old, lives under the shadow of Tara.

Joe, Anne & Francis Ledwidge, Janeville c.1912
(*courtesy of the National Library of Ireland*)

# FRANCIS LEDWIDGE
# AND HIS POETRY

*Padraic Colum*

FRANCIS LEDWIDGE'S is the poetry of the plain – specifically of the demesne land that is the County Meath. The land is beautiful under the light that gives its fields the greenness of jade, but it has scant variety of interest: fields, hedgerows and streams; larks, blackbirds, and pigeons, with a castle or an ancient ruin among ivy-enwreathed trees are what the eye of a poet would mostly note there. There are villages and people, of course, but the poet I have just been re-reading might not approach the people unless they grouped themselves as people in an idyll.

He has been compared to Robert Burns, because his poetry came out of country life as seen through the eye of a young man of the soil. But Francis Ledwidge saw country people and saw the country not at all in the way that Burns saw them. Indeed, his genius was at the other side of Burns's – it was idyllic where Burns's was dramatic; Francis Ledwidge responded not to the tumult but to the charm of life; it was his triumph that he made us know the creatures of his world as things freshly seen, surprisingly discovered. The first poem in his first volume let us know the blackbird's secret:

*And wondrous impudently sweet,*
*Half of him passion, half conceit,*
*The blackbird whistles down the street.*

He finished the stanza with the line 'like the piper of Hamelin', and spoiled it with a literary allusion. Too often, indeed, he gives us the hieroglyphics of literary tradition. It was the fault of a young country poet who had something of the hedge-school in his culture, but it was a fault that he would, most likely, have got away from – 'When will was all the Delphi I would heed', 'Aeolus whispers to the shadows', 'Like Jason with his precious fleece anigh the harbour of Iolcos'. He discovered for us the blackbird's secret and he showed us the mystery that is in the snow-winged flight of herons:

*As I was climbing Ardan Mor*
*From the shore of Sheelan lake,*
*I met the herons coming down*
*Before the water's wake.*

*And they were talking in their flight*
*of dreamy ways the herons go*
*When all the hills are withered up*
*Nor any waters flow.*

He did not attempt to conquer new forms, but he restored their graces to old ones. In 'To a Linnet in a Cage', 'The Homecoming of the Sheep', 'A Little Boy in the Morning', and 'The Herons', he has left us lovely poems.

I have said that his genius was at the other side of Burns's. It was idyllic and akin to the genius of Theocritus. Indeed, Francis Ledwidge was the Sicilian singer of our day, and it is probable that he would have made the discovery that Theocritus was his master.

I kept for a long time a letter that I had from him. It was a letter written in a small back-sloping handwriting the winter before the Great War and was headed 'Janeville, County Meath'. I had a notion that Janeville was a cottage, rose-covered, and just off a country road. But I never saw Ledwidge's home. I had told him that I had never been at the Boyne in Meath, and had never seen the Brugh of Angus. His letter was to tell me that would meet me at a place near his home and be my guide to the Brugh. I never made the journey with him.

Then I saw him – it was for the last time – at Christmas. I met him in a street in Dublin with a writer whose death, like Ledwidge's, is an irreparable loss – the writer of *The Weaver's Grave*. We went to the back of a coffeehouse to have a talk. Francis Ledwidge had been out of Ireland for a while – he had been in Manchester, I think – and he was going back that evening to his home in Meath.

I well recall his big frieze overcoat and how – although he had no thought of entering the army at the time – he looked like a young lance-corporal. He was a big-boned, ruddy-faced, handsome youth. He was boyish and eager that evening but with something of a drift in his mind. He had no notion of what he wanted to do with himself. The *Saturday Review* and the *English Review* were paying him four or five guineas for poems. He was pleased that he could show us he was getting such sums. All very well, but what was he going to do for a living? He had worked in a shop in Ireland and he had been doing something in England. These things were now over for him. Even the profession he was working to acquire – engineering – seemed too prosaic. I felt that he had a boyish notion that he might become a Byron and live magnificently on the sales of the books he was about to publish.

Silly stories were current about his origin and his employments. There was a suggestion that he was hardly literate. The publishers of his *Songs of the Fields* informed the world that he had been a scavenger on the roads. Nothing of the sort. He struck me as the sort of boy who might have belonged to a good Irish farmer family. His education was probably better than the education of an American youth who has been through the ordinary college. I know he had been only in a National school in a country place. But the National school with all its drawbacks is – or was – capable of giving a boy a good literary education. It is because the eighteenth-century ideal still lingers in our country that such stress up to a while ago was laid on literary culture, and in many National schools an effort was made to give it. The old sixth book that a boy took two years to get through made for an exceptionally good training in English, and we may be sure that Francis Ledwidge got all the benefit of it. I remember hearing that as a little boy he had been found crying on one of the school benches. The boys in the class near him were reading aloud from *The Deserted Village*, and he had been overcome by the sound and suggestion of the verse.

Lord Dunsany was Francis Ledwidge's great neighbour, and Lord Dunsany had made himself talked about on account of his enthusiasm for imaginative things. It was to Lord Dunsany that Ledwidge took his first song-offerings. The elder poet helped him with his verse, eulogized him in Dublin, and influenced the important London reviews toward publishing his poems. This intervention put the youth of twenty with the poets of the day. For all this Francis Ledwidge had a personal loyalty to Lord Dunsany – the loyalty that the simple-hearted young Irishman always gives to the leader who captures his imagination. His entering the army was, I think, an expression of personal loyalty. At the opening of the war he joined the Inniskillings, the regiment in which Lord Dunsany was captain. Perhaps too, the adventure he once sung of in the poem called 'After My Last Song' drew him:

*I want to see new wonders and new faces*
*Beyond East seas; but I will win back here*
*When my last song is sung, and veins are cold*
*As thawing snow, and I am grey and old.*

He did see wonders 'beyond East seas', for he served two years with the Mediterranean force in Gallipoli or in Saloniki. 'I am in France', he writes in a letter that I have, a letter dated 11/7/17. 'I have been on active service for two and a half years, and France is the third front I have fixed my bayonet on.' Later he was flung into Flanders, where he became a casualty.

What the world now has of him is but his first song-offerings; the whole of his personality had not come under his control, and his verse-technique was not yet perfected. Let us be critical and say he was unvarying and that he was immature. But we shall have to say too that in everything he wrote there was the shapely and the imaginative phrase. He wrote about simple and appealing things and he wrote about them in a way that leaves them for us as glimpses of beauty – 'Haw-blossoms and the roses of the lane', 'Spring with a cuckoo on either shoulder', 'Maids with angel mien, bright eyes, and twilight hair', 'The bloom unfolded on the whins like fire'. He knew the fields and the hedgerows and he knew their haunters. Has anyone told us more about the blackbird, the magpie, the robin, or the jay-thrush?

*And wondrous impudently sweet*
*Half of him passion, half conceit,*
*The blackbird whistles down the street ...*

*Above me in their hundred schools*
*The magpies bend their young to rules...*

*And here the robin with a heart replete*
*Has all in one short plagiarized rhyme.*

And now I shall quote one of the poems that appeal to me most. How fresh it is! In it are the Irish fields, and the heart of a youth who knew them well.

*The Living Age*, 8 November 1924

## TO A LINNET IN A CAGE

When Spring is in the fields that stained your wing,
And the blue distance is alive with song,
And finny quiets of the gabbling spring
Rock lilies red and long,
At dewy daybreak, I will set you free
In ferny turnings of the woodbine lane,
Where faint-voiced echoes leave and cross in glee
The hilly swollen plain.

In draughty houses you forget your tune,
The modulator of the changing hours.
You want the wide air of the moody noon,
And the slanting evening showers.
So I will loose you, and your song shall fall,
When morn is white upon the dewy pane,
Across my eyelids, and my soul recall
From worlds of sleeping pain.

Seán Dunne & Trish Edelstein, Janeville October 1988
(*courtesy of Trish Edelstein*)

# A COTTAGE IN MEATH

*Seán Dunne*

TO PASS the time when in Dublin lately, I went through the housing estates of Finglas and took the road north to Monaghan, out past Ashbourne where a big monument commemorates an engagement between Republicans and the British in 1916. Driving along a road that curved and straightened through the lush landscape of what FR Higgins called 'our most lovely Meath', I came at last to the village of Slane. It has the look of an English village about it, with its bridge and castle at the edge. There wasn't much stirring. I drove near the partly gutted mass of Slane Castle which looks like a real castle, the way a child would dream of it.

Two women hitch-hikers stood at the side of the road, their tanned faces hinting at the south of France or Spain. A man with a cap low over his forehead wheeled past on a bike. I turned right at the village and took the road towards Drogheda. Everywhere signposts pointed to the passage graves of early Ireland: Knowth, Dowth, Newgrange. In the distance I could see the Hill of Tara. On a hill in Slane Saint Patrick is said to have lit the paschal fire. Everywhere Irish history lies beneath the landscape like lining beneath a carpet.

It was then I came to Francis Ledwidge's small cottage, set on the side of the road in the centre of the Boyne Valley, just a half mile from the village. His cottage is still preserved as a small museum to his memory, and to see it there with its door open and the brick around it the colour of some dark wine, was to stumble on a delight.

On a shelf one can see a rusty shell case from the First World War with, standing inside it, a small statue of the Virgin Mary: prayer within death. Here and there in the cottage are his books and letters, his fiddle and his photograph. This is where he lived as a boy. This was home.

> *A burst of sudden wings at dawn,*
> *faint voices in a dreamy noon,*
> *evenings of mist and murmurings,*
> *and nights with rainbows of the moon.*

Walking around the little cottage, I thought it the kind of place where a man would have no choice but to be a poet. The day had all the ingredients of romantic poetry: a book of poems by Keats on a shelf; the sun in the garden; Ledwidge's fiddle near a fireplace; his neat bedroom where an anachronistic modern electric fire gives out heat; a big stone where Ledwidge and Ellie Vaughey, the woman he loved, met when the stone was on her farm nearby.

> *A blackbird singing*
> *on a moss-upholstered stone,*
> *bluebells swinging,*
> *shadows wildly blown,*
> *a song in the wood,*
> *a ship on the sea.*
> *The song was for you*
> *and the ship was for me.*

Ledwidge's cottage is a simple, scrubbed place. And Ledwidge wrote simple poetry of sunsets and spider-peopled wells. It is the kind of poetry that is uncomplicated and haunts people who might never read a poem at all. It puts him in the ranks of those whose poems, while being somewhat less than great, will always be more than minor and never less than memorable. My own favourite among his poems is 'June'. Lots of people probably learned his 'Lament for Thomas MacDonagh' in school:

> *He shall not hear the bittern cry*
> *In the wild sky, where he is lain,*
> *nor voices of the sweeter birds*
> *above the wailing of the rain.*
>
> *Nor shall he know when loud March blows*
> *thro' slanting snows her fanfare shrill,*
> *blowing to flame the golden cup*
> *of many an upset daffodil.*
>
> *And when the Dark Cow leaves the moor,*
> *and pastures poor with greedy weeds,*
> *perhaps he'll hear her low at morn*
> *lifting her horn in pleasant meads.*

A few of the letters on show in the cottage are from Lord Dunsany who discovered Ledwidge's talent and made contact with London publishers who brought out his work. Looking at the letters, I caught here and there a hint of master-and-servant patronage, but Dunsany seems genuinely to have appreciated the worth of Ledwidge's poems. And to see the poems as Ledwidge wrote them, pinned in glass cases in the cottage, one can see immediately what Dunsany, who was himself a successful writer, would have found in them.

Ledwidge joined the British army but his soul, he said, was by the Boyne, 'cutting new meadows'. Everything that makes Ireland complex and complicated and heartbreaking comes together in him: influenced by the cadences of English verse, he lamented the death of an Irish rebel; he sang the praise of his native landscape but died, wearing a khaki uniform, in another country under another flag. Standing in the childhood cottage, I thought that Ledwidge was no longer enigmatic but had become for me an image of the spirit of poetry and the very opposite of what the business of poetry can involve. His memory and example connect with an enthusiasm for poetry. He symbolizes the pure note.

Seamus Heaney has written of him in his poem 'In Memoriam Francis Ledwidge':

> *In you, our dead enigma, all the strains*
> *Criss-cross in useless equilibrium*
> *And as the wind tunes through this vigilant bronze*
> *I hear again the sure confusing drum*
>
> *You followed from Boyne water to the Balkans*
> *But miss the twilit note your flute should sound.*

As I stood in the garden of Ledwidge's cottage, I heard bees among the flowers. Trees were in leaf and now and then a car zipped past. Otherwise, it was a picture of peace, the kind of house where a man might lean on a half-door for ages and watch the leafy countryside without a care. It was far from the trenches of the Somme and Ypres, and from the grave where Francis Ledwidge lies, among scores of other dead soldiers, in a First World War cemetery near Ypres:

> *The moon leans on a silver horn*
> *above the silhouettes of morn,*
> *and from their nest-sills finches whistle*

*or stooping pluck the downy thistle.*
*How is the morning so gay and fair*
*without his whistling in its air?*

Dead at thirty, Ledwidge never made it among the major poets. Like John Hewitt (whose conservative forms he shares), he paced his thoughts by the natural world. His poetry is not layered enough to read too often and it does not reveal deeper meanings with time. It is old-fashioned, for sure, but his importance for me lies as much with what he represents as with what he produced. And what he represents ultimately has little to do with questions of national identity. On that morning in Meath, reading those old manuscripts, I found myself restored again to a proper sense of his presence and to the clear fact of his gift.

# FRANCIS LEDWIDGE'S
# COTTAGE  ❈  *Seán Dunne*


I remember his small poems, country
intimacies in fading ink;
an old fiddle, books, a small
Virgin set in a shell from the Front.
In the garden, bees seemed from a page.

It became the measure of what followed,
a day of devoured happiness,
our breaths in the dark of tumuli
crossing in a single cloud.
Nothing again could ever live up to it.

In a photograph we stand at the door,
your hair in the wind, my beard that's shaved.
We could be some couple looking for roots
at the homestead where it all began,
heady with achievement of a moment's grace.


from *Collected* (The Gallery Press, 2005/2015)

Drimpale St

Sir.

As per instructions I have examined shore on 83 (as reported by Mr Law) and as far as I can see blockage does not occur under the road. There is a bank four feet in breadth between the mouth of the shore and the quick on the roadside: in my opinion blockage occurs there, as the shore is open on the roadside to take off water from road which office it seems to fulfil perfectly, while the water from the field is but slowly trickling from under the bank to this opening.

The shore on 99 ( as reported by Mr Smith ) is laid with six inch pipes and capable of taking all the water which comes down the pipe. If it has failed to act it is by reason of the people directly opposite erecting a permanent dam where the water made its exit from the shore. I have got this dam taken down and the water subsided shortly afterwards.

Your obedient Servant
Francis Ledwidge.

J Quigley Esq.

Undated letter to County Surveyor James Quigley
(*courtesy of the Francis Ledwidge Museum*)

# RATHFARNHAM TO JANEVILLE: IN THE POET'S FOOTSTEPS

*Richard Ball*

I HAVE little doubt that the short journey from his bed to the back door of Daly's grocery shop in Rathfarnham, was the hardest, if not actually the longest, part of Francis Ledwidge's famed walk through the night to his home in Janeville. Alice Curtayne imagines the young poet stepping silently down the stairs and unlocking the back door. Dermot Bolger sees him carefully making his way across the dark and cluttered shop floor. I like to think of the enormous sense of relief and liberation the fifteen-year-old must have felt, at least momentarily, when having quietly closed the door on a future career in retail, he breathed in the fresh night air of Rathfarnham and set off north for Slane. It was to be his long night's journey into day.

Curtayne estimated the distance at thirty miles, Dermot Bolger has it at nearly forty. Informed by satellite, my watch tells me that it is 32.57 miles to the gate of the cottage and the distance can be covered walking, with short breaks, in under ten hours.

I had for quite some time intended to retrace the young poet's footsteps of 1903. On 10 April of this, his centenary year, following as precisely as possible the documented route taken by Ledwidge, I did just that. There were some differences of course. Whereas my walk was done in daylight, he walked through the night without the benefit of modern runners, tracksuit and a light backpack. Unlike me, he had no access to cafés, shops and service stations along the route, although I only used them for take-away coffees. I carried a small amount of food and water which was sufficient for the day. I also had the company of a friend for the first five miles, and of another for two miles through Ashbourne.

We stood in the middle of Rathfarnham village near The Yellow House, once Daly's Shop, in the pre-dawn and looked around. At this hour it was easy to imagine ourselves in the quiet night time streets of more than a century earlier. It was easy too to imagine the young Ledwidge hurrying at first to put some distance between himself and his former employer. We were in no rush but nevertheless set out at a steady pace at exactly 6.05am. We headed up Rathfarnham Road, on to Terenure Road then through Harold's Cross towards Christchurch. It was an idyllic morning, the moon imperceptibly giving way to the sunrise. One road of beautiful red brick houses (which had no on-street parking) looked very much as it would have when the young fugitive made his escape along it all those years ago.

At Christchurch we veered left, then right, down Winetavern Street through the heart of Viking Dublin and the scene of the battle to save Wood Quay which has now itself become part of the city's history. As we crossed the Liffey my focus was on the pedestrian lights and the busy morning traffic. Had I looked upriver I would have seen James Joyce Bridge on Usher's Quay and, on the south side facing the bridge, the house which is the setting for his most celebrated short story 'The Dead'. In 1903 the bridge was exactly 100 years in the future and 'The Dead' had not yet been conceived. But Joyce had already met George Russell (AE) who would be instrumental in having his first short story 'The Sisters' published the following year. A mere seven years on, the same George Russell would introduce a promising young poet named Francis Ledwidge to man of letters, poet, dramatist and fellow Meath man Lord Dunsany.

Less than an hour and about three and a half miles, and we were already making our way up Constitution Hill. The city is smaller than we think. Passing Doyle's Corner we went on through Phibsborough with Dalymount Park on our left. I remembered the 1970 F.A.I. cup final replay when the legendary Al Finucane lifted the trophy for his native Limerick for the first time. Three years later another Limerick man, Daniel 'Don' Givens scored a hat-trick, (another first) in a sensational victory over Russia in a European qualifier. Memory and myth combine.

If the young Slane boy had looked left in the darkness, he might have made out the shape of a corrugated iron fence that surrounded a pitch that would become a part of football folklore and the home of Irish soccer in the decades to come. Home to Bohemian FC for over a hundred years, when the young Ledwidge walked passed Dalymount in 1903 it was only in its infancy as a football ground. Originally common land with a large vegetable plot known as Pisser Dignam's Field, it was taken over by Bohs who hosted the first game there (versus Shelbourne) on 7 September 1901. Less than two years later it was chosen as the venue for the final of the Irish Cup played on 13 March 1903, very close to the presumed date of the poet's walk. In 1904 it hosted its first international between Ireland and Scotland.

Bohemian's founding members were largely past pupils of Clongowes Wood and Castleknock College and home games were originally played at the Polo Grounds in the Phoenix Park. Different times indeed! Of the earliest players, six were medical students, all of whom would qualify as doctors. In fact one of the clubs most auspicious players was a doctor. Oliver St John Gogarty, who played for two seasons between 1896 and 1898, was however more famous as an author, poet and one-time friend of James Joyce. Joyce immortalised him as the character of Buck Mulligan in *Ulysses*. Oliver St John Gogarty and Francis Ledwidge came from opposite ends of the social spectrum yet, within a decade of the penniless young poet's long walk home, they would be well acquainted, having been introduced by a mutual friend Lord Dunsany. Gogarty was one of two writers (AE was the other) who shared a life-long friendship with the literary lord. They died within a month of each other in 1957.

Whatever about the corrugated iron fence, there was nothing unusual for the fifteen-year-old to notice as he walked past a row of houses opposite Dalymount Park. He could not have known that in one of the houses in St. Peter's Terrace a 44-year-old woman lay terminally ill. May (Murray) Joyce, mother of James, would be confined to bed until she died on 13 August 1903, a year to the day before the publication of her prodigious son's first short story. Born in Terenure in 1859 (we had passed her place of birth less than an hour earlier) she is buried in Glasnevin Cemetery. Leopold Bloom, in a different book and another time, might remark "a puzzle to cross Dublin without passing a Joycean landmark".

If Ledwidge had looked right as he crossed the canal towards Glasnevin, he would not have seen, as we did, Croke Park. Home to Gaelic Games for over a century and another monument to memory and myth, in 1903 it was still merely Jones' Road Sports Ground and had been home to Bohemians FC from 1893 to '95. It was not until 1913 when it was purchased by the GAA that it was given its now revered name, by which time the name of Francis Ledwidge was already being written into our literary history.

Following his route, we moved on. After a quick Americano at a Topaz service station in Glasnevin, my companion and I parted ways. Before he walked back into town to get on with the business of the day (it was still not eight o'clock) he told me that he would visit the famous cemetery to pay homage to one of its equally famous residents, Gerard Manley Hopkins, who is buried in a communal Jesuit plot to the left of the main front gate. The young Slane poet passed within a few yards of the remains of one of the great poets in the English language, unaware, as were most people, of his existence. On that night in 1903 Hopkins had been dead for fourteen years, yet it would be another fifteen before, in 1918, a year after the death of Francis Ledwidge, his collected poems would be published for the first time. The twenty-nine years between the death of Hopkins and the publication of his poetry coincides almost exactly with the twenty-nine years of Ledwidge's short life. Apart from a poetic gift, both also shared a distaste for the Dublin that they both worked in, the one for five years, the other for not much more than five days. I like to imagine that something of the poetic soul of Hopkins touched the fledgling poet as he passed in the darkness. Lines from 'The Windhover', had they been available to him, might have encouraged the young Slane boy to soldier on,

> *... sheer plod makes plough down sillion*
> *Shine*

Fortified with caffeine, I made my way on towards Finglas against the general flow of cars, bicycles and pedestrians. It was a beautiful bright morning but, as forecast, I was heading directly into a cold northwest wind. What kind of weather did the young runaway have to endure? I approached Finglas with some excitement. Curtayne tells how Ledwidge drew companionship from the Royal Mail milestones along the road to Slane and how he used them to estimate the distance covered and what remained. Dermot Bolger located the milestone in Finglas over sixty years later, and sat on it, eyes closed in anticipation of his own personal pilgrimage to Janeville. Bolger, who has assimilated the Ledwidge narrative into his own, has become almost synonymous with the

Slane poet who inspired and validated his venture, against the odds, into the world of words. If a Slane road worker could be a poet, why not a lad from working class Finglas. Bolger nailed his colours to that particular mast when as a sixteen-year-old he spent his savings and bus fare on the biography of his hero and walked home to Finglas. I thought of that walk too as I approached the suburb which still has the feel of a village about it. Although I didn't see the milestone I felt I had arrived at one, having traversed the city, a distance of seven miles, in under two and a half hours. One more obstacle and I would be liberated onto familiar country roads. Better the devil you know.

Having found my way under the M50 and negotiated the flyovers, cycle paths and walk-ways, a maze of metal and mesh, that took me over the M2, I stepped down into a sort of industrial outpost where the N2 that I had driven so often on my way to Croke Park or Dalymount dissolves into weed and wasteland. Slightly disorientated and disconcerted it brought to mind T. S. Eliot's great poem and the line

*I will show you fear in a handful of dust.*

Whatever fears Francis Ledwidge felt on his long night walk, the young boy already more than halfway through his short life would experience far worse wastelands than this in his final three years. Born in 1888, Eliot was just a year younger than Ledwidge yet lived till 1965. Waste is a word that comes to mind.

Having covered exactly eight miles and placed a significant barrier between myself and the city I celebrated with half a chicken sandwich and within a couple of miles began to recognise a once familiar road. From there to Ashbourne would double the distance I had already walked. Long straight stretches into a cold and constant north-west wind without the variety of the city streets made for tedious progress. Three and a half miles every hour, seven miles in two, and plenty of time to do the maths. There was little variation, little to encourage a quickening of the pace. But I plodded on looking forward to getting to Ashbourne, passing Balrath and finally arriving in Slane. It was just a matter of time, and patience became the primary virtue.

A second coffee and a short break at a service station about three miles from Ashbourne were a relief and a distraction. Young Ledwidge had no such little luxuries. I also had the promise of a friend's company through the south Meath town. A sign announcing that I was crossing the county boundary gave me a bit of a lift, as did the second half of my sandwich. Approaching Ashbourne it was good to see a friendly face on the outskirts. We chatted our way through the town and half a mile beyond. Then he returned to his work and I headed on into the longest straightest stretch of the journey.

What did Francis Ledwidge think about through the long night hours and on those long straight miles? I thought of everything, anything and nothing. But mainly nothing. The sheer monotony of taking one step after another for hours on end, somewhere in the region of fifty or sixty thousand steps in total, is a mental more than a physical challenge. Physical discomfort was confined to my feet which, by the final third of the walk, had swollen in my snug fitting runners. I considered phoning my wife and asking her to meet me at Balrath Cross with a fresh and slightly bigger pair. I can't imagine that young Frank's shoes or boots were designed for this kind of distance. He had no phone, so I decided not to use mine.

I wonder if the darkness made the long stretches easier for Ledwidge. The constant traffic noise was one thing he didn't have to deal with. Whatever traffic he did meet would have been horse-drawn bringing supplies to the city and empty carts and wagons on the homeward journey. Was he offered a lift? I was, by someone who recognised me, about 4 miles from Slane. I remembered how our hero was mistaken for a poacher as he hid, out of embarrassment perhaps, from the postman until the bailiff recognised young Frank Ledwidge. Likewise I recalled how the aforementioned Dermot was mistaken for a burglar until he established, as he writes, his 'bona fides as a literary pilgrim'. I was merely mistaken for a man slightly deranged. I declined the offer of the lift. By then I was too close to give up. But tedium was a constant for me and no doubt for the fifteen-year-old boy walking home through the night with his first poem in his pocket. Did he recite it on the way? I did, several times.

> *Above me smokes the little town ...*

And I dreamed forward to that final climb of the journey when the words would become real and I would be just half a mile from the back garden in Janeville where I intended to sit as Frank did and savour the sense of having arrived. This, for me, would be the end of a long-promised journey that had taken decades to realise.

Near Balrath Cross two men are strimming a bank clean of bright yellow blooms and I think of Kavanagh's beautiful

> *Dandelions growing on headlands, showing*
> *their unloved hearts to everyone.*

The great Monaghan poet and his Meath counterpart had more in common than their humble rural backgrounds. Neither had any formal education beyond primary school level but each had a strong bond with a mother who was ambitious for her offspring. Both for a time worked the land, but more than that they loved the landscapes that nurtured their growing. Like Hopkins, neither of them took to Ireland's capital. In 'Self Portrait' Kavanagh describes his coming there as the greatest mistake of his life. He too made the long walk to, rather than from, Dublin and we can well imagine Ledwidge having written Kavanagh's

> *There will be bluebells growing under the big trees*
> *And you will be there and I will be there in May;*
> *For some other reason both of us will have to delay*
> *The evening in Dunshaughlin ...*

Indeed it is easy to see Kavanagh composing these as he sits in the back garden in Janeville among the abundant bluebells, so in sympathy are they with the spirit of the place and that of the young Meath poet. Kindred spirits certainly, Ledwidge's 'moss-upholstered stone' becomes Kavanagh's 'green stone lying sideways in a ditch'.

When Patrick Kavanagh was born in 1904, Francis Ledwidge was just sixteen. They lived, literally, within walking distance of each other. Drumlin country is just a few miles north of Slane. Kavanagh was eleven years old when Ledwidge's first collection *Songs of the Fields* was first published. He was thirteen and still at school in 1917 when the young Slane poet was killed at Ypres and his second collection *Songs of Peace* appeared. It is not impossible that, like Dermot Bolger over half a century later, the young boy from Inniskeen heard for the first time the inspiring 'Lament for Thomas MacDonagh' read to him by his teacher, and to the same effect.

Curtis's service station/shop about five miles from Slane provided me with my third coffee. The young man who served it asked how far I had walked. "27 miles," I said, having checked my watch. He told me that he was preparing with a group from the parish to walk the Camino in Spain, so I think he understood what I was up to. A little further on I was offered the aforementioned lift by a friend from Essex, now settled in Meath, who is familiar with both the Ledwidge story and the cottage-museum. Having turned it down, the last four miles became increasingly harder. This was partly because I knew that I had refused the option of sitting into a comfortable car seat and being transported to Slane in five minutes. But also, ironically, as the end comes into sight, figuratively speaking, patience runs out rapidly.

Curtayne tells us that 'he sighted Slane on the horizon as the sun was rising'. I was watching in anticipation of this moment, and it arrived. Over the crest of a rise in the road was the view that Ledwidge had slogged through the night to see. The hill of Slane with its ancient ruins came first into sight. A quarter of a mile further on, across the still-hidden valley of the Boyne, the road pointed directly towards the cottage in Janeville. Depending on trees and foliage at the time it is possible that from two miles distance, before the mill, before the castle woods, before the road rising to the village came into view, young Frank Ledwidge could see his own home.

*And scenes of old again are born ...*

Down the hill, over the Boyne, steeped in myth and history, and up the steepest of hills. Left at the crossroads brings one towards Navan. One can imagine an exuberant young Frank speeding downhill on his bicycle which he calls 'Pegasus', a new poem in his pocket, on his way to visit his great friend Matty McGoona in the neighbouring town. But that imagining will come later. Just now speeding is not a concept I can readily conjure up so turning right I shuffle up the final rise out of the village on the road to Drogheda.

The distance can now be measured in hundreds of yards. So I start counting my steps. Did he do likewise? I walk on the soft grass verge outside the village to give my burning feet some relief. I keep counting and very soon the end is in sight, literally. There it is, the cottage/museum with its little car park (a modern necessity). At the gate I check my watch for time and distance; 15.51pm and 32.57 miles respectively. As planned, I sit on the first bench in the garden on the right and read the lines that propelled the young poet home;

*I walk the old frequented ways ...*

And I realise that I just have. As a student I worked in London in the summer of 1975, the same year the sixteen-year-old Bolger, biography under his arm, walked home to Finglas and found the famous milestone. In my rucksack I packed, and not for the last time, the collected poems of Patrick Kavanagh and of Francis Ledwidge. They were then my quiet companions. Have been ever since. I have often sat beside the life-sized likeness of Kavanagh on the seat beside the Grand Canal for a quiet chat. I knew that I owed it to myself and to Ledwidge to accompany him on his long solitary walk through the night.

Maybe time is not linear and neither of us walked alone. And maybe an eccentric lord, fond of walking and of writing and of ghosts of other days, added a third party to an odd couple sitting on an old Royal Mail milestone somewhere between Rathfarnham and Finglas and Slane.

I look back over the valley to where I'd stood half an hour previously and enjoy the moment of rest in the late afternoon sun. Then I walk further up the garden to 'the moss-upholstered stone' and imagine bluebells growing under the big trees. It is time, finally, to go inside.

I suspect that Frank and his twelve-year-old brother Joe went in by the back door, but the sign asks visitors to enter by the front, as visitors usually do. I lift the latch and it makes that distinctive sound, that familiar double click that Francis Ledwidge would have known as well as he knew his mother's voice. I step inside and whisper, under my breath, to myself, "I'm home."

# ASCENSION THURSDAY, 1917

Lord, Thou hast left Thy footprints in the rocks,
That we may know the way to follow Thee,
But there are wide lands opened out between
Thy Olivet and my Gethsemane.

And oftentimes I make the night afraid,
Crying for lost hands when the dark is deep,
And strive to reach the sheltering of Thy love
Where Thou art herd among Thy folded sheep.

Thou wilt not ever thus, O Lord, allow
My feet to wander when the sun is set,
But through the darkness, let me still behold
The stony bye-ways up to Olivet.


Sent by Ledwidge from the Western Front
on 31 May 1917 to Katharine Tynan

# FIFTY YEARS AFTER

## Eavan Boland

TOWARDS THE end of his life Yeats attempted to define the difference between the English and Irish traditions. It was a difficult procedure, for great Irish poetry had only just come into being and he was its cradle. Any definition was bound to be limited to his own experience and he himself admitted this when he wrote: 'I know what I have tried to do, little what I have done.' Yet he contributed a magnificent and intuitive distinction between the two traditions when he suggested that the Irish temper in poetry was quicker, more tuned to crisis. To the English tradition he ascribed a different quality: 'The English mind is meditative, rich, deliberate; it may remember the Thames valley.' Thinking of Wordsworth's composed and conscious retrospect, of Spencer's elaborate patience, of Milton's symmetry, and measuring these against Yeats's own urgency of praise and protest one can only concede his point and wonder at its wisdom.

The anomaly of Francis Ledwidge is that, while he was a direct contemporary of Yeats and his countryman, his sensibility has more of deliberation in it than crisis; his imagery recalls English serenity rather than Irish outcry. His imagination, in its steadfast choice of what is innocent and native, could almost be a changeling of the Thames valley.

All this has resulted in a confused estimation of his work. The anthologies inevitably display those short lyrics of his which coincide with a show-case patriotism. But Ledwidge was not a patriot in the Irish sense of that word. He had a generous awareness of vicissitude and injury in Ireland, but this did not deter him from joining the British army in the Great War. In his assessment of the place which nationality has in poetry, he coincides more nearly with the English than with the Irish poets. For the Irish it is part of that crisis out of which, as Yeats suggested, they draw their inspiration; for the English it is part of that peace which Yeats ascribed to their poetry – 'rich, meditative, deliberate'. For of course – for reasons of history – nationality in England has remained an assumption, whereas in Ireland it has always been a commitment. There is no reason to think that Ledwidge made that commitment. Part of the joy of his work is that he was equipped to praise this countryside in a style without social indignation. Ireland was his Muse, not his cause.

He was born in Meath in 1887 and was educated at the local national school. Information about his boyhood and youth is scarce, and in any case they seem to have been uneventful. One thing, however, must be said: it is ungenerous in retrospect to question Dunsany's perception and treatment of Ledwidge, once he became his patron. Nevertheless, Dunsany's constant affirmation that Ledwidge had vindicated his opinion of the Irish peasantry is naïve where it is not tedious. For example, in his introduction to *Songs of the Fields*, Dunsany wrote: 'If one has arisen where I have so long looked, for one, among the Irish peasants, it can be little more than a secret that I shall share with those who read this book.' Any condescension in Dunsany is undoubtedly outweighed by his generosity, nevertheless Padraic Colum's recollection of Ledwidge is more sensible and refreshing: 'He struck me as the sort of boy who ... belonged to a good Irish farmer family.'

Ledwidge was active in his own community. He participated in the dramatic society; he championed the Gaelic League and the GAA and joined the Volunteer corps within some months of its foundation. In 1914, however, he enlisted in the Royal Inniskilling Fusiliers and three years later defended his choice with the words: 'I joined the British Army because she stood between Ireland and an enemy common to our civilisation and I would not have England say that she defended us while we did nothing at home but pass resolutions.'

❉ ❉ ❉

Ledwidge's poetry is divided into three sections. The first is *Songs of the Fields* which consists of his earliest work, written from the age of sixteen until 1914. The second is *Songs of Peace* which contains the poetry of two years, from 1914-16, among it the famous lyrics on the insurrection. Finally, there are the last songs which comprise thirty-three slight and, one suspects, unfinished pieces composed between 1916 and his death in 1917.

All in all, his poems are probably the work of no more than seven or eight years. And when one comes to state the chief reservations about his achievement it has to do with just this. For his poetry does not develop in such a way that one suspects the poet of having a vision with urgent and inevitable powers of growth. The economy, the exquisite imagery, the pastoral allegiance are there from start to finish but they remain static like the green sights they express. There is no great stride from acorn to oak in Ledwidge, as there is in Keats's poetry.

All this comprises Ledwidge's strength as well as his weakness. If his work lacks the scope of ambition, Ledwidge is always an immediate delight; there is nothing unintelligible, nothing of the over-reacher in his response to what he sees. He has no wish to learn or to instruct; he looks for no moral just as he communicates no riddles. This self-sufficient joy in the mould of objects rather than their meaning made him at times a perfect reporter of natural beauty. It also reduces his stature. As a poet of the countryside he has moments of greatness; but as a spirit he lacked curiosity.

Ledwidge triumphs when he can be directly descriptive and since description is his gift, his victories are confined more often to the single line than to whole poems. For example, he writes of a spring day with 'ground winds rocking in the lily's steeple', and in the same poem he discovers a magical personification for April:

> And she will be in white I thought, and she
> will have a cuckoo on her either shoulder ...

When he joins his lyric gifts with effects of philosophy or of a literary derivation, he fails. His rhythms falter and his control over beauty evaporates like scorched dew.

But when he maintains a style of direct observation, then his images are uniquely accurate. For instance, he begins one poem with an incomparable cry of delight: 'Come, May, and hang a white flag on each thorn/ Make truce with earth and heaven.'

❉   ❉   ❉

It has been said that Ledwidge's debt to Keats is too heavy for his poetry to be considered apart from its source. Naturally, this results in the conclusion that Ledwidge is the inferior poet and the comparative too frequently becomes an absolute: too often Ledwidge is subsequently considered inferior. It may be useful then to his reputation, not to compare him with Keats but to contrast him for a change and to show that he was more simply a *yes* nature poet than Keats ever was or wished to be.

Keats's gift for catching nature in 'a strong toil of grace' has no peer. He wrote for instance of 'Mid-May's eldest child/ the coming musk-rose' and of the abundance of Autumn but these visible objects directed him to an invisible world. Keats used nature to explore his own spirit in a way Ledwidge never could. For Ledwidge the countryside provided a crowd of sights to be praised and caught in images; for Keats it provided insights. Where Ledwidge found natural beauty alone, Keats discovered a meaning which transcended the natural world while it could only be expressed through it. The difference in their outlook is confirmed in a passage from one of Keats's letters when he speaks of nature in such a way that leaves no doubt he discovered there a presence Ledwidge had no access to:

> *What astonishes me more than anything is the tone, the colouring, the slate, the moss, the rock-weed; or, if I may say* *Keats* *so, the intellect, the countenance of such places. The space, the magnitude of mountains and waterfalls are well imagined before one sees them: but the countenance of intellectual tone must surpass every imagination and defy any remembrance.*

But if Ledwidge never found such majesty and if this confirmed his style and status as poet, yet it gives his work a unique beauty as well. He discovers lesser identities in nature than Keats did. That is to say, Keats discovers himself through the natural world and so joins vulnerable humanity to changeless nature as in the *Ode to Autumn*, while Ledwidge simply found before him what was green and natural and already master-minded, and looked no further. The quintessence of this is contained in his loveliest poem *The Wife of Llew*. In it two characters, in an act of friendship, decide to make a mate for Llew out of whatever is fresh and perfect in Spring. They build her face out of field-flowers and construct her feet on the span of a bird's wing. It is a vision of perfection. — *indeed!!)*

*The Irish Times*, 31 July 1967

# THE WIFE OF LLEW

And Gwydion said to Math, when it was Spring:
'Come now and let us make a wife for Llew.'
And so they broke broad boughs yet moist with dew,
And in a shadow made a magic ring:
They took the violet and the meadowsweet
To form her pretty face, and for her feet
They built a mound of daisies on a wing,
And for her voice they made a linnet sing
In the wide poppy blowing for her mouth.
And over all they chanted twenty hours.
And Llew came singing from the azure South
and bore away his wife of birds and flowers.

# LEDWIDGE'S LANDSCAPES

*Gerard Smyth*

WHEN FRANCIS Ledwidge was preparing to go to what he called 'the great battlefield', he wrote from Richmond barracks in Dublin to Lizzie Healy in the Meath village of Wilkinstown: 'It is spring now and it must be lovely down in Wilkinstown. Are the birds singing yet? When you hear a blackbird think of me.' I reached for those wistful words to use as an epigraph to my own poem, 'The Blackbirds of Wilkinstown'.

Throughout his war, that homesickness for his Meath landscape continued to occupy his thoughts and define much of his writing. While the title of a poem such as 'Serbia' might imply a war theme, placing the soldier-poet by Lake Dorian in Macedonia where he contemplates the 'sudden glories of the dawn / Shine on the muddy ranks of war', his thoughts remained 'full of Ireland's old regret'.

When I think of Ledwidge I see him in the summer fields and on the tree-lined roads or standing at one of the ancient sacred sites of the county, not as a trench-warrior at the flash-points of the Balkans or Flanders, where he died one hundred years ago. Unlike his fellow poets whose writing entered a new phase as a result of the war – Sassoon, Owen, Rosenberg, Graves, David Jones or the Germans, Benn and Trakl – his experiences in 'the muddy ranks' did not yield poems that placed him among their ranks.

*... the homeways ...*

Unlike his fellow countryman, the Kerry poet Thomas MacGreevy, it was as if both his temperament and lyric vocabulary had no accommodation for the imagery war offered, much less the existential truths and broken humanity that surrounded him in no-man's-land. The poetry of his years in the Great War does not reveal a witness to its horrors and bleak vistas but a soldier preoccupied by memories of home and consumed by his longing for 'the great peace of the homeways', as he wrote to Lizzie on another occasion.

The simplicity of home and singing its praises overshadowed all else; in his devotion to his arcadia he is, perhaps, matched only by Rupert Brooke and his 'foreign field / that is forever England':

> *Her sights and sounds; dreams happy as her day;*
> *And laughter, learnt of friends; and gentleness,*
> *In hearts at peace, under an English heaven.*

> (from Brooke's 'The Soldier' )

Nor is there any attempt in Ledwidge's poetry to explore or articulate his moral cause or the sense of moral obligation that derived from his conviction that Britain 'stood between Ireland and an enemy common to our civilisation and I would not have her say she defended us while we did nothing at home but pass resolutions'.

An event that did bring a charge to his poetry was, of course, the failure of the Easter Week rebellion in Dublin and, especially, the execution of its leaders. Not only did it provide his best-known and most resounding poem, 'Thomas MacDonagh', it contains an acute sense of his subject that he seemed unable, or unwilling, to summon to develop poems that incorporate more fully the degraded landscape and implications of the first World War into his imagery.

Had he survived, his poetry – clearly maturing in both style and substance on the evidence of a number of the later poems – might well have reflected on those moral issues as well as engaging with the treatment that his fellow soldiers received on returning from the trenches and the silence forced upon them; haunted men who had to lock away their ghosts. In 'Soliloquy' he foresaw the fate of the forgotten thousands of Irishmen who sacrificed their lives:

> *A little grave that has no name,*
> *Whence honour turns away in shame.*

Could it have been that Ledwidge shared what Yeats expressed as 'a distaste for certain poems written in the midst of war':

> *I think it better that in times like these*
> *A poet's mouth be silent, for in truth*
> *We have no gift to set a statesman right...*

('On Being Asked for a War Poem', WB Yeats)

Yeats, of course, stood at a cosy distance from the actual battlefields and was probably thinking of a certain kind of armchair war poetry. Although Ledwidge was embedded in the fullest experience of war, his biographer Alice Curtayne maintained that he 'contributed nothing to war poetry as such', that even in the midst of war his 'allegiance was to nature and repulsion from the conflict'.

On the other hand, Seamus Heaney in his rigorous introduction to a selection of Ledwidge's poems, places him as a war poet in the company of Owen and Sassoon, and poet and war poetry anthologist Jon Stallworthy included him in his *Twelve Soldier Poets of the First World War*.

Despite his immersion in some of the epic moments of the Great War – the slaughter of Gallipoli and a test of endurance in

wintry Serbia – Ledwidge only partially fulfilled what he seemed
to promise in his poem 'In the Mediterranean – Going to the War':

> *In my soul a steadier will,*
> *In my heart a newer song.*

The stimulus to this 'newer song' was not the war-torn
landscape and its potent metaphors or the dramaturgy of battle
and death. Instead, a number of his lyrics are notable for the way
in which they imaginatively draw on scenes that had an obvious
appeal to what Heaney called his 'tender-heartedness', as well as
his keen sense of place – 'Evening in England', 'Autumn Evening
in Serbia', 'The Home-Coming of the Sheep'. These poems and
others bear out Curtayne's contention that nature and not war
remained his theme.

Even when he fleetingly looks to his wartime situation, the
language he uses remains close to the quasi-mystical idiom of his
pastoral poetry: in 'The Irish in Gallipoli' he tells us, '... we but war
when war / Serves Liberty and Justice, Love and Peace'. When he
very occasionally allows the war to interrupt his reveries of home,
it seems only a vague awareness of what is all around him: 'the mad
alarms / Of battle, dying moans and painful breath'.

> *The Present is a dream I see*
> *Of horror and loud sufferings.*

His images rarely take any fuller account of those loud
sufferings; instead his imagination drifts back to the peaceful
settings of his Meath landscape. Recuperating among the maimed
and wounded in Egypt he sees only 'the bluebells swinging' and
hears 'the blackbird singing', and in 'Skreen Cross Roads', also
composed while recovering in Egypt, the poet returns to a place
where 'One road sings of the valleys green / Two of the sea and
one of the town...'

MacGreevy, on the other hand, opens his eyes to a different and apocalyptic landscape:

*The earth is snow-white,*
*With the gleam snow-white answers to sunlight,*
*Save where the shell-holes are new,*
*Black spots in the whiteness –*

*A Matisse ensemble.*

*The shadows of whitened tree stumps*
*Are another white.*

('De Civitate Hominum')

Even in letters to friends Ledwidge tends towards lyrical description rather than any portrayal of catastrophe – 'the shrieking iron and flame' and 'Poppies whose roots are in man's veins' that Rosenberg saw at break of day in the trenches. Writing to editor Edward Marsh, he speaks of the German rockets as having 'white crests which throw a pale flame across no-man's-land and white bursting into green and green changing into blue and dropping down in purple torrents. It is like the end of a beautiful world.' Ledwidge, it seems, even in war can find a kind of beauty in the drama.

In the interludes between bombardment and battle, he takes pleasure in the pastoral and in remembering his Meath landmarks. Writing to the poet Katharine Tynan in June 1917, only weeks before his death, he tells her:

*Although I have a conventional residence I sleep out in the*
*orchard ... You are in Meath now, I suppose. If you go to Tara,*
*go to Rath-na-Ri and look all around you from the hills of*
*Drumconrath in the north to the plains of Enfield in the south,*

*Whoa!*

*where the Allen Bog begins, and remember me to every hill and wood and ruin, for my heart is there.*

Again to Marsh, the following month:

*even as a big strafe is worrying our dugouts and putting out our candles, my soul is by the Boyne cutting new meadows under a thousand wings and listening to the cuckoo at Crocknaharna ...*

Even in what we might call a *bona fide* war poem, and one of Ledwidge's most striking as well as being a prophetic final poem, 'A Soldier's Grave', he moves from the battlefield's 'mad alarms', 'dying moans, and painful breath', to a description of the grave being in a place where 'the earth was soft for flowers' and 'the lark shall turn her dewy breast'.

Ledwidge left us songs of the fields and songs of peace but no true songs of war.

We can only speculate as to the kind of poems his songs of the aftermath of war might have been but I suspect he might have looked back, as Robert Graves and others did, and produced an altogether different and transformed poetry born out of the experience, as well as out of his responses to the forces at work in post-independence Ireland.

Dublin, March 2017

## THE BLACKBIRDS OF
## WILKINSTOWN ❖ *Gerard Smyth*

*It is spring now and it must be lovely down*
*in Wilkinstown. Are the birds singing yet?*
*When you hear a blackbird think of me.*

Ledwidge, in a letter to Lizzie Healy, 18 February 1915

There's a village where nothing has changed for years,
sweet pastures through which the railway track
is a memento kept as part of the scenery;
the bog where bog work was a tug-of-war
and Ledwidge's blackbird flaunted her song.
The gatekeeper's cottage is gone, no need now
for the gatekeeper's morning and evening vigil.
The trees are like trees in a Russian novel –
tall and gaunt, some ready to fall
in the next winter storm. The righteous
have their inner sanctum: the country chapel
where they pray for the bride at the altar,
the soul in the box. No spectacle ever intrudes
except when the blackbirds arrive.
Through the sweet pastures, meeting ground
of the harriers, it's a short walk
from schoolhouse to cemetery where husbands
and wives are resting in peace
and stone walls keep a little of the sun's day-warmth
for night that comes darkening the harvested fields.

from *The Yellow River* (Solstice Arts Centre, 2017)

# IN MANCHESTER

*John McAuliffe*

WHEN WB Yeats heard about the insurrection in Dublin in April 1916, he was staying with his artist friend William Rothenstein near Stroud in Gloucestershire. It was there that Yeats, after the kind of cajoling and prompting which were part of the process for some of his greatest poems, began to write 'Easter 1916'.

Francis Ledwidge also responded to the Rising, though from a very different English base, a requisitioned primary school, Lily Lane, in Moston in Manchester. After serving in Gallipoli and Serbia where he was injured, he was sent to Manchester to be treated. The Western General Hospital here had expanded into various primary schools which were re-constituted as hospital wards, which is how Ledwidge ended up in Lily Lane School in 1916.

I drove up there on 27 March last, on the same anniversary day that 'A Nation's Voice' was being beamed out of a bedraggled Collins Barracks in Dublin. The identical wet, cold weather had descended on North Manchester and the streets around the school had the hatless look of any treeless part of a city. When Ledwidge was there, he was able enough to go out walking and visited a sister who lived not too far away. The experience, though, did not endear the area to him (and he may also have been remembering

Manchester as the city to which his sometime muse Ellie Vaughey had moved when she married).

'In Manchester' offers a predictable response to being housed in the industrial north: 'There is a noise of feet that move in sin / Under the side-faced moon here where I stray.' Opposed to his present confinement is a dream of the Boyne:

> *I often think my soul is an old lie*
> *In sackcloth, it repents so much of birth.*
> *But I will build it yet a cloister home*
> *Near the peace of lakes when I have ceased to roam.*

It is easy to imagine how a crowded requisitioned school, with 216 beds, some in the classrooms but others in the cobbled school basement, would have made a 'cloister', anywhere, a more attractive prospect.

As the Rising began on 24 April 1916, his imagination began to focus with more particularity and vividness on this cloister he could 'roam' in, centring on how it was also a world dreamed up by his friend Thomas MacDonagh, critic, poet, lecturer and revolutionary.

 Ledwidge's elegy for MacDonagh, written after he learned of his execution, is more adventurous than many of his other poems, as it tries to draw MacDonagh's work and death into its pastoral scene. MacDonagh's best-known poem had been his translation of an Irish-language drinking song, 'The Yellow Bittern', and as a critic he had written with wit and clarity about the possibilities of carrying some Irish-language poetic techniques across into Ireland's long English-language poetic tradition.

Ledwidge's poem, drafted in that Manchester school-turned-ward, alludes to the thirsty bittern in its opening lines and to an Irish-language image for Ireland as a lost cow in the closing stanza, while his medial rhymes give the poem great assurance. But Ledwidge does not hand over his poem to MacDonagh's technique and arguments about the Gaelic mode. The tight quatrains and more expected pastoral images, those Wordsworthian daffodils (growing in the schoolyard when I visited it and outside my south Manchester window as I write this), co-exist with these stranger, national images.

Twelve months later, back in action, and a long way from yellow bitterns and dark cows (and Slane and Dublin and Manchester and Stroud), on a rainy summer day, Ledwidge died near Ypres. 'Thomas MacDonagh' would be published that same year in his second, final collection, *Songs of Peace*. That wet afternoon in Moston, there were just a couple of traces of Ledwidge and the poem he would write.

When he was there the area had already begun to decline: there was less activity in the printworks and dye and bleaching works which had once made this part of the city prosperous. The run-off and waste from sand pits made up an artificial landscape. The area did send large numbers of troops to the Front, although Ledwidge is not the Irish soldier most associated with that. Major Henry Kelly was the same age as Ledwidge, was born in Dublin but raised in Moston and it is through him that Moston remembers the war. He received the Victoria Cross for 'most conspicuous bravery in attack', and the Military Cross for 'gallantry and devotion to duty'.

But what is just as striking about Kelly is his post-war life, as a member of the Free State's 'National Army' and in the 1930s as a volunteer in the International Brigades in the Spanish Civil War where he received the Laureate Cross of Saint Ferdinand, before rejoining the British Army, aged 52. Kelly retired to Manchester and died here in 1960, having lived, like Ledwidge, a life of more than one allegiance.

Ledwidge in Manchester was between worlds, a man writing non-commissioned poems, *in media res*, while the countries he had known re-assembled around him. His position and his boldness and his commitment to artistry, are part of why he has become a way for us to think about the past, and how it continues to rise up among us a century later.

Manchester, March 2017

## LEDWIDGE IN
## MANCHESTER  ✠  *John McAuliffe*


Having made mincemeat of his shoulder, he convalesces,
not knowing, but – really – *knowing* that some Father
will sooner rather than later record he was blown to pieces
stopping in out of the drumming rain for a cuppa

with his unit ... In Ypres. A different unit
to the one he has left in the Balkans, for the upset assembly
around him in Lily Lane, in the schoolroom they've had to refit
as a men's ward, so national is the level of casualty.

This is in the run-up to Easter in 1916.
Outside he can be seen observing the new daffodils
bending under the northwest wind. It's been and gone.
The not much that lies ahead of him, and helpless symbols.

*Irish Life* 10 August 1917: Joe, Francis & Anne Ledwidge,
and Jimmy 'The Buckley' Cassidy, Janeville c. 1912,
(*courtesy of the National Library of Ireland*)

# THE BRIDGE OF THE BOYNE
# FRANCIS LEDWIDGE:
# POET IN A MINOR KEY

*Peter Fallon*

IT IS my hope this afternoon* to give a personal account of my encounter with, and abiding interest in, the poetry of Francis Ledwidge. As the title might suggest, the Boyne being the principal river of County Meath where I grew up and where I have lived almost all my life and where Ledwidge was born in 1887 and lived until he went to war in the British army, I have some affinity with him, his work, and an interest in his fate. I'm aware, of course, that my mention of a poet in a 'minor key' in my talk's subtitle isn't likely to pack a room. But in an age of hyperbole perhaps we make too many claims that X or Y is a major figure, great or the greatest. I'll return to my idea about 'minor' and I'll hope to suggest a case for its worthiness too.

It may be that a poet's obscurity is best demonstrated or confirmed when there's no sign of him or her in the site or source where you might most confidently expect to find it.

The Belfast critic Edna Longley published her *Poetry in the Wars* in 1986. There is no mention in this collection of essays of Francis Ledwidge, who enlisted to serve in the First World War, wrote poems that have fixed themselves in people's affections, and died at the Front before he was thirty. As we approach the centenary of the 'Great War', and a mere three years later the centenary of

Ledwidge's death, this may be a fitting time to remember him, to reconsider what must be seen as an unfulfilled promise.

For a river that's a mere 70 miles long the Boyne enjoys, and endures, a singular reputation. It rises in the Bog of Allen of County Kildare and meanders most of its way through County Meath before it enters the Irish Sea in County Louth. It passes through Trim, near Tara, ancient seat of Ireland's high kings where St Patrick appeared in 433, through Navan and Slane, the village beside which Ledwidge was born. It is a river with a fabled past. On its banks are the majestic megalithic monuments of Knowth and Dowth and the apogee of art and architecture from that age, Newgrange, edifices all that pre-date the Pyramids of Egypt and cast a spell still.

The Boyne Valley includes Kells, whose monastic settlement is linked to Ireland's most famous book and beside which I grew up, and it includes Loughcrew where my home is and on whose small hills – we call the biggest of these the 'mountain': in a county as flat as Meath you make the best of every bump in the road – is an assembly of thirty cairns, that include passage graves, from the time of Newgrange, that is two-and-a-half or three thousand years BC.

It was from a well that was charmed into overflowing to become the Boyne itself that Fionn MacCumhail, we're told in a tale of legends from the 7th-14th centuries, tasted the fish that fed on hazelnuts that fell into it and became the Salmon of Knowledge.

For some, the Boyne conjures nothing more readily than the battle that took place there in July 1690 though they think of it as though it were yesterday and tally the wounds inflicted and suffered.

Historians here will know more about this than I but they'll agree, I trust, that the Battle of the Boyne, the war of two kings, a clash between the armies of Catholic James and Protestant William, William of Orange, though not decisive in itself was a turning –

literally a 'reverse' – in Catholic fortunes and spurred victories for William the following year in Limerick and, conclusively, at Aughrim.

It ensured the Protestant Ascendancy, especially in the North of Ireland, and prompted and fuels the annual marching season there each summer. (When James, incidentally, abandoned his Irish supporters he gained a nickname of indelicate directness: Seamus a Cháca, James the Shit.)

But the 'bridge' of the Boyne? Well, there are several – at the towns I've mentioned, near Rosnaree where Ledwidge courted one of his doomed loves and dreamt of high kings:

> *And one said: 'A loud tramp of men*
> *We'll hear again at Rosnaree.'*
> *A bomb burst near me where I lay.*
> *I woke, 'twas day in Picardy.*

The bridges include one that carries the Dublin to Belfast motorway and the viaduct at Drogheda that bears the same cities' interrail track.

I know the river more intimately than many. I have paddled most of it, and all of its tributary, the Blackwater, in an open canoe. But by 'bridge' – indicator of a means to ford some place, a connecting point, perhaps I mean most of all a line or lead to a previous time.

Soon after I returned to make a home in County Meath I found myself thinking about Francis Ledwidge and trying to imagine what his life was like, what it was like to be born into a cottage in County Meath in the late 19th century, to be born into a life of the deprivation that followed his father's death when Ledwidge was a boy, that left his mother a widow with her several young children. I tried – and I failed.

Until, that is, I came to know a man who was born in the same year as Ledwidge, 1887, though he outlived him by sixty-five years. And by another coincidence this man shared his name with Ledwidge's godson, one Thomas Ward.

But to all of us, Tom Ward whom I used to visit in the cottage in which he grew up in Farranaglough, 'The Field of the Stones', and who took me first to see The Speaking Stones was the 'Conny' Ward, Conny from cunning – Scots, ken – knowing, clever.

Now Conny lived in an uncommon arrangement. He'd sold his cottage to a couple who came from nearby, who'd live a lifetime in America and who retired and returned to live near their home place. And their agreement had been that Conny could stay in the house with them for the rest of his days. He was in his late 70s at the time and, I'm guessing, they thought those days mightn't be many. But Conny had other ideas and he told me one evening that they'd 'buckets' of money and he'd lie awake in the night hoping they'd leave it to him when they died!

Although I'd encountered nursery rhymes and other verses before I went to boarding school I have vivid memories of the first three poems I encountered in a maroon schoolbook in Mr Maher's English class at St Gerard's, near Bray in County Wicklow. One was an extraordinary juggling act of rhyme and rhythm by – I learned later – an oddball called T E Brown who wrote sometimes in the Manx dialect, that is of the Isle of Man, hardly a man with an appetite for an audience. It was called 'My Garden', written in 1893, and it went like this:

> *A garden is a lovesome thing. God wot!*
> *Rose plot,*
> *Fringed pool,*
> *Ferned grot –*
> *The veriest school*

*Of peace; and yet the fool*
*Contends that God is not –*
*Not God! in gardens! when the eve is cool?*
*Nay, but I have a sign;*
*'Tis very sure God walks in mine.*

I remember I liked the sound of it – its skip and hop – and I probably sensed even then that its formal shape and patterns obscured or overbalanced its thinking, whatever idea it hoped to promote or convey.

Another poem which fixed itself in my mind was John Masefield's 'Cargoes' with its ornate vocabulary and exotic points of reference.

*Quinquireme of Nineveh from distant Ophir ...*

Had I a clue what that meant? And its courageous juxtapositions of the

*Stately Spanish galleon coming from the Isthmus ...*

The what! And the

*Dirty British coaster with a salt-caked smokestack*
*Butting through the Channel in the mad March days ...*

It was decades before I learned that its author, a Poet Laureate of England, when asked once about the history of shipping, shrugged off complaints that Nineveh was, in fact, two hundred miles inland.

And the third of these first poems was one called 'The Home-Coming of the Sheep':

*The sheep are coming home in Greece,*
*Hark the bells on every hill!*

*Flock by flock, and fleece by fleece,*
*Wandering wide a little piece*
*Thro' the evening red and still,*
*Stopping where the pathways cease,*
*Cropping with a hurried will.*

*Thro' the cotton-bushes low*
*Merry boys with shouldered crooks*
*Close them in a single row,*
*Shout among them as they go*
*With one bell-ring o'er the brooks.*
*Such delight you never know*
*Reading it from gilded books.*

*Before the early stars are bright*
*Cormorants and sea-gulls call,*
*And the moon comes large and white*
*Filling with a lovely light*
*The ferny curtained waterfall.*
*Then sleep wraps every bell up tight*
*And the climbing moon grows small.*

Curiously, it was years before I made a connection between this poem's author's home and where I lived, the landscapes we both knew, the riverbanks we'd walked. I might hardly have known its author's name and hardly, even, whether he was Irish or English, so schooled were we still then in the literature of England. The Mediterranean setting of the poem probably inhibited any palpable notion of a local connection. But I know I responded again to the steady march of its lines, probably paused at that arch 'Hark' in the second line – or indeed maybe I *didn't* because we expected such language – *God wot!* – and poetry to include, even to be built on, such quirky ingredients. I suspect I couldn't have recognized those sheep as ones like the crossbred Suffolks in our flock near Kells. We'd no bells on ours – and shepherds' crooks were even then a thing of past times. But if these three stanzas conjured a foreign land and distant scene, one image registered with me for its gorgeous clarity – 'The ferny curtained waterfall' – and, in the same poem, one word stopped me in my own tracks, that 'cropping' with a hurried will. I knew that stealthy act, the hesitant, daring pause as sheep were being driven out of a yard, unable to resist the temptation to snatch a stalk of timothy or rye, and the risk worth taking of being snapped at by a suddenly sniping, crouching Border collie. It warmed me some years ago to find in one of Ledwidge's letters the following: 'So you liked the poem about the sheep? So do I, very much.'

Only one familiar, even intimate, with country ways would use that word, 'cropping', so naturally. And it is precisely that kind of finely focussed eye for detail that I came to treasure as I learned more of Ledwidge's poetry. Its music, image and atmosphere appealed to me then and have continued to engage me.

And yet in recent years especially I've found myself thinking more and more about the waste of his life and, inevitably, about the what-might-have-been. We can but speculate. And I find myself thinking, while remembering his art's nature and range and prospects, about his poems' comparative silence, their indirect reference at least, about that cataclysmic episode of his time, the almost unthinkable horrors of what we still call the 'Great War'. How is it, I ask, how his themes and tones don't match in their outrage the protest of his contemporaries, some of whom also met their fate in the same gruesome conflict. Yes, he wrote 'A Soldier's Grave' but where is his 'They' or 'Base Details' of Siegfried Sassoon, his 'Anthem for Doomed Youth' – 'What passing bells for these who die as cattle . . . ' – or the nightmare vision and report of 'Dulce Et Decorum Est' and 'Strange Meeting' of Wilfred Owen?

Let me come back to this.

Let me try, first, to put his art and gift in a context. What we have are a young man's poems. He was not yet thirty when he was, as he predicted he might be, 'hauled beyond life'.

But while he was an individual and the author of distinctive, lasting verses, his poetry – it should go without saying – didn't exist on its own. It was part of a tradition – an amalgam of inherited folk compositions and a learned literary line. Much of this learning came from the access granted by a patron to the library of a castle nearby and resulted from his entrée to the fringes of Irish literary life as brokered by the same enthuser.

As he noted, mere months before his death, he never met Yeats – and his elaboration of a wish to is interesting and telling:

> *'I have never met Yeats but I hope to one day for I have much to say to him . . . I don't think he has ever quite reached the hearts of the people – [for which there might have been a good argument] – and if any of his works live it will be early poems on Maeve and Cuchullain – [for which there surely isn't].*

Just how attentively the progenitor of a whole literary, cultural and national movement, founder of the Abbey Theatre, future Nobel Laureate and author already of 'No Second Troy', 'September 1913', 'Easter 1916', and the collection *Responsibilities* might have listened to 'The Blackbird' of Slane is, again, something we can only estimate. But it's likely we'd estimate accurately.

It would be remiss, I believe, to think or talk about Francis Ledwidge without acknowledging the support and help he received from Edward Plunkett, better known as Lord Dunsany and well-known in his time as a writer of fantasy. Dunsany, of both

Catholic and Protestant ancestry – on the Plunkett side was Oliver, the Primate of Ireland, who was born, it is said, in Loughcrew where his family certainly had a dwelling and cornmill in the field that adjoins my home, who was martyred at Tyburn in 1681 and canonized in 1975, the first Irish saint in almost 700 years. Joseph Mary Plunkett, executed in 1916 after the 'Rising', was also related.

Dunsany associated with Yeats, Lady Gregory and the Abbey Theatre. Like many of his caste he was an army man. He served in the second Boer War and the First World War where he was wounded. Though an officer, he experienced the Front Lines. But for all this, his enduring legacy may be his support for Ledwidge and, later, another writer whose earliest stories link her to the Boyne.

Ledwidge wrote to Dunsany in 1912 and they met soon afterwards. Though I don't believe they could have known each other well – they came from such different social divisions – Dunsany agreed to help the young poet and succeeded in securing publication of his work and wrote introductions to his books. He failed, however, in dissuading Ledwidge from 'joining up' – he even offered financial support – and by another coincidence they served in the same unit.

Years later Dunsany found himself at the end of a similar request for help with literary advice – this time from the father of Mary Lavin who went on to become the doyenne of the Irish short story. In his introduction to *her* first collection, *Tales from Bective Bridge*, a bridge of the Boyne, he writes with characteristic generosity:

> *I have had the good fortune to have many stories and poems sent to me by young writers. In nearly all of them the ardours of youth showed flashes, some rarely, some frequently, but in only two of them have I felt sure that I was reading the work of a master. And these two great writers, as I believe them to be, both*

*wrote to me by a strange coincidence from the same bank of the same river, the left bank of the Boyne. One of these writers was Francis Ledwidge, who unhappily lived too short a time to do much more than show promise of the great bulk of fine work of which I am sure he was capable . . .*

*I now have the pleasure of introducing another fine writer, Miss Mary Lavin; very different from Francis Ledwidge, except for the same piercing eye, which to Ledwidge revealed the minutest details of Irish hedgerows, with all their flowers and birds, and to Mary Lavin the hearts of women and children and men . . .*

*When Ledwidge first brought his work to me I gave him a very little advice, which he immediately profited by, as people do not usually profit by advice. The best thing I did for him was to lend him a copy of Keats; and the great speed with which he seemed to absorb it, and slightly to flavour his work with it, gave me some insight into his enormous powers, which were unhappily never developed. But my first impression when Mary Lavin sent me some of her work, an impression that I have never altered, was that I had no advice whatever to give her about literature; so I have only helped her with her punctuation, which was bad, and with her hyphens, about which she shares the complete ignorance that in the fourth decade of the twentieth century appears to afflict nearly everybody who writes.*

Indeed Dunsany's thoughtfulness in opening the doors of his library to the young poet is a pointer to the unheralded patronage that was often the practice of the landed gentry and owners of Big Houses. It must have been around the time that Dunsany was announcing Mary Lavin to the literary world that John McGahern, a boy then still, benefitted from similar kindness. Though impoverished then, in comparison with Dunsany, the Moroneys, Willie and his son Andy, members of a family that was 'riding on the rims', as we say, and eccentrics both – they became models for the Kirkwoods in some of John's finest stories. But by opening their library at the Rockingham Estate they granted McGahern what he has called his early education.

As often as not, Ledwidge's earliest poems, in common with others of that age – he was, after all, still a teenager – were as true to the *ideal* of a life as to life itself.

Formally they adhered so closely to tired models that you knew when and where to expect a stress or rhyme and, as is so often the unfortunate case, when that stress or rhyme arrived, at the very expected juncture, it was also the stress and rhyme you expected.

Dunsany, in his introduction to Ledwidge's first book – in which introduction he'd no hesitation about branding Ledwidge a 'peasant' poet – while celebrating his fluent melody, pinpointed the jaded phrases and hollow notes in the notebooks he was working from. Sometime Ledwidge simply tried too hard:

> *And pearly droppings of the dew*
> *Emberyl the cobwebs' greyness.*

There are antique constructions,

> *July I feel*

and archaic words he uses and attempts to play with, such as 'jade', as in 'tire', be jaded:

> *Who will not weary of waiting, or jade*
> *Of calling to me for aye.*

In a poem, 'Last May' – 'I went to meet my love at dark' – he introduces the words 'wold' and 'fen', neither of which are part of his landscape or language. They belong to the south of England (wold) or east (fen, the Norfolk fens), though fen has established itself in New England, and notably in Boston's Fenway.

He can be cloyingly sentimental – see 'Desire in Spring':

*I love the cradle songs that mothers sing*
*In lonely places when the twilight drops,*
*The slow endearing melodies that bring*
*Sleep to the weeping lids . . .*

But he succeeded in discovering and asserting a distinctive voice. Sometimes this shows in the plain fixture of a word or phrase – for instance, that 'cropping with a hungry will'. He writes of the 'holy water of the rain', describes June as 'a nomad gipsy' (think Irish weather), and the 'shallow brook' his tuning fork and the birds 'my master'. In 'To One Dead' the blackbird, recurring creature and symbol, sings on

*a moss-upholstered stone.*

A windy evening

*drops a grey*
*old eyelid*
*down across the sun.*

Even a conventional poem, such as 'To One Dead' which I've just cited, is suddenly informed by an engaging riddling quality:

*A blackbird singing*
*On a moss-upholstered stone,*
*Bluebells swinging,*
*Shadows wildly blown,*
*A song in the wood,*
*A ship on the sea.*
*The song was for you*
*And the ship was for me.*

*A blackbird singing*
*I hear in my troubled mind,*
*Bluebells swinging*
*I see in a distant wind.*
*But sorrow and silence*
*Are the wood's threnody,*
*The silence for you*
*And the sorrow for me.*

Sometime the hallmark signature effects derive from something more adventurous, a rhyme that's slightly off,

*View thee / beauty,*

and a few lines later

*begs of us / Pegasus.*

And sometimes there's a formal adventure or breakthrough. In truth I don't know if it's a breakthrough that makes 'To a Blackbird on a Sign-Post' so beguiling. I mean, I don't know if the poem's rough-hewn effect is the result of being unfinished or the successful result of a gamble he took composing it. But in this poem it's the unrhymed line in each verse that catches and clings to our attention.

*Here drift the ways apart, and nomad winds*
*Whisper like old men on the centre-piece*
*Of ravelled fringes, or like comrade hinds*
*Take a short leave and whistle down the roads,*
*Some with a lightsome heart and some with loads*
*Of grief and heavy minds . . .*

*And in that light I hear again your song*
*Echoing from the ears of every cliff,*

> *And see the panting fox tongue hanging long*
> *Out of the torn hedge, whose broken ways*
> *Are safely guarded as Thermopylae's*
> *By Spartan briars strong.*

In 'Thoughts at the Trysting Stile' the longer lines stretch Ledwidge to deeper thought and clearer observation. By removing the safety net of each rhyme and metronomic rhythm he galvanizes a reader's interest and attention on his high-wire flight.

I've read and heard little or nothing about Ledwidge as an influence on poets who came after him. But by extending and enlivening the old Irish tradition of *dinnseanchas*, that is, the lore of places/placenames, the notion that a landscape lends itself to being read, Ledwidge by now truly responsive to a familiar world anticipates Patrick Kavanagh as a laureate of local places. He lists Currabwee, Skreen Cross, Crewbawn and Stanley Hill a generation before Kavanagh imprinted Inniskeen, Shancoduff, Mucker and the stony grey soil itself of Monaghan as key points of a literature's atlas. Indeed Ledwidge's fanciful ditty, 'The Fairy Man' with its specific Crocknaharna Hill,

> *Go back, Tim Farley*

and

> *Cooney's sheep*

prefigures much that the author of 'The Great Hunger' and *Tarry Flynn* etched on our consciousness.

Ledwidge's 'the moon from the well in the lane' in 'Lullaby', or 'she makes her life one long beatitude' ('In the Garden') and 'when Moses made a laneway in the sea' would not be out of place in the work of the later writer, author of 'In Memory of My Mother', 'Epic', 'A Christmas Childhood' and the sonnets that signalled his rebirth of the banks of the Grand Canal in Dublin.

It's impossible to imagine that FR Higgins, who also moved in Yeats's circle and who was appointed by Yeats as Managing Director of the Abbey, and whose home Higginsbrook was also on the banks of the Boyne, didn't know Ledwidge's poetry well.

His 'Father and Son' is imbued with the same lyric quality.

> *Only last week, walking the hushed fields*
> *Of our most lovely Meath, now thinned by November,*
> *I came to where the road from Laracor leads*
> *To the Boyne river – that seemed more lake than river,*
> *Stretched in uneasy light and stript of reeds.*

The range and weight of influence on Ledwidge is notable especially in his renderings of ancient Irish myths, derived (we may assume) from the repossessions of folk material from a Gaelic world by Standish O'Grady and Douglas Hyde, particularly the latter's *Love Songs of Connaught* (1893), in the same way that at the same time the young Austin Clarke mined the same material in his *The Vengeance of Fionn* (1917), a retelling of episodes in the narrative of the pursuit of Diarmuid and Gráinne, and in the way Clarke mined Jacobite songs for his entrancing lyrics 'The Lost Heifer' and 'The Planter's Daughter'. Ledwidge's masterpiece perhaps, his elegy for Thomas MacDonagh – and, we could say, for himself – perfects the adoption of metre and assonance from old Irish poetry before Clarke dared to employ them.

In Ledwidge's poem 'The Herons', which commemorates a visit to an old encourager at Lough Sheelin (and I like to think that as Ledwidge made his way from Janeville outside Slane to this lake, he took the road that passes my home), in 'The Herons' more than the bird that goes on ...

> *dreamy ways*
> *when all the hills are withered up*
> *nor any waters flow*

... connects this poem with Yeats's magisterial, mysterious song, 'The Stolen Child', published in *Crossways* in 1899 and one of the few essential Yeats poems written before he was the age at which Ledwidge died.

Even Joyce's poems in *Chamber Music* (1907) play and replay the same Georgian notes, themselves repetitions and echoes of Elizabethan romantic lyrics, as Ledwidge's early offerings. But it was the difference in these authors' natures – Joyce's and Ledwidge's – that prompted one into the inventive broadside of 'Gas from a Burner' in tones imponderable in the Meath poet's gentle lines.

But none of the unevenness I've been describing should surprise us. It all happened so quickly. And it is part of the complex fate of Ledwidge's life and times and professional decision.

In a poem, which in Alice Curtayne's *Collected* follows one addressed to his mother, Ledwidge writes of his muse, 'She read no book', she 'never heard of Babylon or Troy'. His own learning about books and near mythical places is reflected in the journeys he took – first cycling to work in a mill every morning and back home every evening, and, later, inconceivably longer and more arduous trips from the 'old frequented ways', the woods and hills and streams in peaceful Meath, from the Boyne's banks, marching to the rumble and slaughter in the Front Lines of Serbia, Gallipoli and the Western Front:

> *from the rapt attention to the song the robin sang to the cacophony of bombs and mortars, the roar and anguished complaints and cries of the dying.*

It's a fact, there are references in his poems to that awful conflict. In 'The Dead Kings' he dreams of Rosnaree – how often his dreams were dreams of Meath – and is woken from a reverie in Picardy in France because as he says with a bold, plain simplicity 'a bomb burst near' where he was lying. 'A Fear' concludes another dream, as if from an afterlife, 'All this thing is hell'; while in 'Serbia', though it mentions 'The muddy ranks' (and that can be understood two ways) of war beside a lake in Serbian Macedonia, the poet, wondering if he could save Ireland, resorts to an *aisling*:

> *I only saw with inner eye*
> *a poor old woman all forlorn.*

It is in his prose, I believe, not his poetry, that Ledwidge's frankest reports take root and his utterances match the passion and directness of his English fellow poets. In only one poem, 'A Soldier's Grave', does he become the voice they were, warning the world, telling the pity.

> *Lest he should hear again the mad alarms*
> *of battle, dying moans, and painful breath.*

In a letter to Dunsany he wrote

> *It was hell. Hell! Not many thought he would return. Just fancy*
> *– out of a company 250 strong, only 76 returned. By heavens,*
> *you should know the bravery of these men!*

To Edward Marsh, editor of an anthology in which his poetry features, he wrote

> *Just now a big strafe is worrying our dugouts and putting out our*
> *candles. (But my soul is by the Boyne cutting new meadows under*
> *a thousand wings and listening to the cuckoos at Crocknaharna).*
> *They say there will be peace soon.*

And he goes on

> *If you visit the Front don't forget to come up the line to see the*
> *German rockets. They have white crests that throw a pale flame*
> *across no-man's land, and white bursting into green, and green*
> *changing into blue, and blue bursting and dropping down in*
> *purple torrents ...*

It's as if he's describing a brilliant firework display – until he corrects, or grounds, the mood:

*It is like the end of a beautiful world.*

Days before his short life ended, at Ypres on the French/ Belgian border, a casualty of a stray shell, he wrote again, in prose, as if he were involved in some wild adventure, not a mortal conflict:

*It was very exciting this time [he was returning from the Front Line] as we had to contend with gas, lachrymatory shells and other devices new and horrible.*

Before, again, he tempers that excitement and ends pro- phetically

*It will be worse soon.*

Why is it that that pitch of reality so rarely surfaces in his poems?

For various reasons. His nature, and the nature of his gift. His aim was song. Sweet music. His was a lyric gift.

But also, I believe, he felt a necessity to seek comfort and consolation for his troubled mind in the imagination, to recreate and to return in his mind to what and where he loved.

*It must be quite beautiful on the bog now. How happy you are to be living in peace and quietude where birds still sing and the country wears her communion dress.*

It was a necessity – as the only way he knew how to endure what he saw, a means of survival.

And third, and again we speculate, there wasn't time. He died too soon and too suddenly for that synthesis to occur, for his impressions to work their way through the mill of his mind and into art.

Dunsany, again prescient, in his introduction to Ledwidge's last poems – a note he wrote from the Hindenburg Line and prefaced with a tone that could only be written by one of his class and officers' rank, comments that he was writing 'amidst rather too much noise [that 'rather'!] and squalor' – observed late in 1917 that, 'If ever an age needed beautiful little songs [and this is a belittling criticism] our age needs them – to soothe the scars of the mind.'

I referred to Ledwidge as a 'poet in a minor key'. I hope by that, first, to assert the musicality of his verses. But I am struck by another possibility when I think of the way his poetry has found its place in the minds and memories of many who mightn't, let's say, call themselves literary people. His poems are remembered and recited.

The opening of his most famous elegy, 'He shall not hear the bittern cry', surprises people by their knowing it. And I wonder if it might be true that there are poets we might 'classify' as *minor* who affect the *hearts* of those who read their work in the way that those we think of as *major* engage and affect the *minds* of those who study them. I suggest that writing that stays with and pleases the *hearts* of local people a century on is no mean thing.

But if I started by suggesting Ledwidge's obscurity and his neglect by some who should admit his right to attention, let me say that he has had steadfast advocates too. Dunsany, of course. Katharine Tynan, who also moved in Yeats's circle, wrote to Ledwidge in the trenches and enclosed an admiring review of his *Songs of the Fields*. Dermot Bolger cites him as a touchstone and has written about him and edited some of his work. Seamus Heaney's *Field Work* (1979) includes a poem in his memory:

> *Francis Ledwidge, you courted at the seaside*
> *Beyond Drogheda one Sunday afternoon.*
> *Literary, sweet-talking, countrified,*
> *You pedalled out the leafy road from Slane*

*Where you belonged, among the dolorous*
*And lovely: the May altar of wild flowers,*
*Easter water sprinkled in outhouses,*
*Mass-rocks and hill-top raths and raftered byres.*

*I think of you in your Tommy's uniform,*
*A haunted Catholic face, pallid and brave,*
*Ghosting the trenches with a bloom of hawthorn*
*Or silence cored from a Boyne passage-grave.*

And there has been no more dedicated champion than Alice Curtayne, an historian who edited the *Collected Poems* and published in 1972 the definitive life.

If I began by suggesting that this point in time, the eve of the centenary of World War I, a few years before the centenary of Ledwidge's death, might be an apt moment to cast a thought or two on him, let me now suggest that this very place might be an apt location for that reconsideration because the first sentence of Alice Curtayne's Acknowledgements reads as follows:

> *My thanks are due to H E John Cardinal Wright who, on a visit to Slane, originally suggested the idea of the biography, by describing the 'Cult of Ledwidge in Boston College, Mass.'*

About that cult I know and have been able to find absolutely nothing. It might be a topic for another day.

---

\* *The Bridge of the Boyne, Francis Ledwidge: Poet in a Minor Key* was delivered on 16 April 2013 at Boston College when the author was Burns Library Visiting Scholar in Irish Studies.

# 'WHEN THE GORSE IS OUT OF BLOOM ...': RECENT IRISH POETRY

*Katharine Tynan*

'WHEN THE gorse is out of bloom kissing is out of favour', runs the old saying, it being understood that on no day of the year is the gorse, or 'furze' as we Irish call it, without a blossom. So with Irish poetry. I think I can remember a time when there was almost a dearth of Irish, as distinguished from Anglo-Irish, poetry. Those were the days of the 1870s and '80s when no young poets were producing anything of account; when Aubrey de Vere, Allingham, and Ferguson were well past their prime; when Todhunter had not found himself as an Irish poet; when Dowden and the Armstrongs pleased the Anglo-Irish ear. I shall provoke controversy perhaps if I say that the Fenian movement produced little, if any, that was not journalistic poetry, although 'Leo' Casey had a very sweet lilt and was indeed a born singer, though too easy and careless to make his poems of real account.

Does anyone remember now the Pan-Celtic Society of the '80s? It produced a good deal of experimental verse in the manner of Hardiman's translations of Irish poetry and Miss Brooke's *Reliques of Irish Poetry*. Most of these translations, though praiseworthy, were in the stilted manner. The eighteenth century lay cold over them all. The day had yet to be for Edward Walsh's liquid numbers, for the golden simplicity of Ferguson and Callanan, the three men who were able to give assurance in the English language of the blackbird note of Celtic poetry. There was also Mangan, of course, who in many ways takes precedence of these three; but Mangan was a translator and sometimes must have improved the Celtic poet.

However, the Pan-Celtic Society, in going back stilted mannerisms of the eighteenth and early Century translations of the Irish bards, rather writing in the English manner, took the first step right way. Then came that consummate craftsman, as well as essential poet, WB Yeats, who led us back to the fountains, to the great clarifying and beautifying of the poetry of that time, and of the time which came after.

The remarkable thing about the poets who came after is that each one, while being distinctive in himself/herself, is yet producing a poetry extremely unlike anything that is being written in England where the war has brought back poetry to her rightful place. As a reviewer of poetry, I believe that hardly any age in English poetry can have produced anything like the quantity of good poetry which is now being written and eagerly read in England. For the war has brought back the ideals.

But to our Irish poets. Take a group of them. AE, like a tree or a mountain, must always be a law to himself. Padraic Colum, James Stephens, Joseph Campbell – have these derived anything of English poetry? I think not. Seumas O'Sullivan, Alice Milligan, Francis Ledwidge, Eva Gore Booth are less distinctively apart; but there is not one of these but has something that is not in the English poetry. That Yeats stands alone, of course, does not need saying. Perhaps those individual poets – exclusive of AE who would have been as he is under any circumstance – might have found their way if Yeats had never been: perhaps not. But his own generation in Irish poetry owed a deal to him.

What an advance we made from the minor English songsters O'Shaughnessy and Philip Bourke Marston, who had never a bush of their own to sing it at all. We have learned since then that an Irish man's or woman's reason for being is to be Irish, to think Irish, to love Irish, to live Irish; and the same is true of other nationalities.

But again to our poets; the last few months have brought us many notable volumes of Irish poetry, some by poets we knew well already, others by younger, less known poets. The youngest of all, Mr Francis Ledwidge, in his new volume *Songs of Peace*, gives us assurance for the succession. Here is a poet as essential as Mr Yeats, endowed with a limpid and beautiful vocabulary, an exquisite sensitiveness, a great sense of beauty, and a most delicate art. When Lord Dunsany discovered Francis Ledwidge, stone-breaking by a Meath road, he had a more wonderful adventure than any of the seekers in his *Tales of Wonder*, and he found a more precious jewel. Francis Ledwidge ought to have been found on a hillside in Greece, a shepherd boy on Latmos, for he has the Greek sense of beauty. From his poem 'A Dream of Artemis', one could take at random many passages which Keats might have written, with a difference. There is more of labouring man: of sorrowing and suffering here than in the Last Arcadian.

> *Though for so short a while on lands and seas*
> *Our mortal hearts know beauty, and overblow,*
> *And we are dust upon some passing wind,*
> *Dust and a memory.*

Everyone who loves poetry will hasten to know for themselves 'A Dream of Artemis'. I will not wrong the beautiful poem by extracting from what is a perfect whole. Here is a lovely thing, fresh as the morning dew.

## A LITTLE BOY IN THE MORNING

*He will not come, and still I wait.*
*He whistles at another gate*
*Where angels listen. Ah, I know*
*He will not come, yet if I go*
*How shall I know he did not pass*
*Barefooted in the flowery grass?*

*The moon leans on one silver horn*
*Above the silhouettes of morn,*
*And from their nest-sills finches whistle*
*Or stooping, pluck the downy thistle.*
*How is the morn so gay and fair*
*Without his whistling in its air?*

*The world is calling, I must go.*
*How shall I know he did not pass*
*Barefooted through the shining grass?*

I do not propose to deal here with the poetry of Thomas MacDonagh and Joseph Plunkett, for the reason that these poets have already been dealt with in *Studies* in separate articles. But I would say that these poets and their fellow idealists have been an inspiration to other poets, and doubtless will continue to be so, since as Lord Dunsany says in his preface to Ledwidge's poems the 'lost cause' has 'an irresistible attraction for almost any Irishman'. Ledwidge in the section called, oddly enough, 'In Barracks' – for he has fought in the war and been wounded and invalided home and gone back again – has a few beautiful poems for the lost cause, of which this is one:

# THE BLACKBIRDS

*I heard the poor old woman say:*
*'At break of day the fowler came*
*And took my blackbirds from their songs,*
*Who loved me well thro' shame and blame.*

*No more from lovely distances*
*Their songs shall bless me mile by mile,*
*Nor to white Ashbourne call me down*
*To wear my crown another while.*

*With bended flowers the angels mark*
*For the skylark the place they lie,*
*From there its little family*
*Shall dip their wings first in the sky.*

*And when the first surprise of flight*
*Sweet songs excite, from the far dawn*
*Shall there come blackbirds loud with love,*
*Sweet echoes of the singers gone.*

*But in the lonely hush of eve,*
*Weeping, I grieve the silent hills.'*
*I heard the poor old woman say*
*In Derry of the little hills.*

James Stephens' booklet *Green Branches* is something very different from the freakish and audacious Stephens we know. *Green Branches* is, unexpectedly and amazingly, an elegy, and written with a high and stately solemnity we have not had before from the poet who has kicked over the conventions of prose and poetry. Listen to this Irish Lycidas:

*Be green upon their graves, O happy Spring,*
*For they were young and eager who are dead;*
*Of all things that are young and quivering*
*With eager life, be these remembered.*
*They move not here, they have gone to the clay;*
*They cannot die again for Liberty.*
*Be they remembered of this land for aye;*
*Green be their graves and green their memory.*
*Fragrance and beauty come in with the green,*
*The ragged bushes put on sweet attire,*
*The birds forget how chill those airs have been,*
*The clouds bloom out again and live in fire;*

*Blue is the dawn of day, calm is the lake,*
*And merry sounds are fitful in the thorn;*
*In covert deep the young blackbirds awake,*
*They shake their wings and sing upon the morn.*

Mr Stephens writes nothing that is not memorable and these noble numbers are worthy of his reputation. Another book of the autumn of 1916 is Miss Eva Gore Booth's *The Death of Fionavar*, a poetic drama, the story being of Maeve, the warrior queen, who is vulnerable through her love for her little daughter. Miss Gore Booth is, as lovers of poetry know, a true and exquisite poet. The latest volume has an added interest because it is decorated by Constance Gore Booth, Countess Markievicz. The designs, especially the wild winged horses, are extraordinarily impressive. Miss Gore Booth's poetry has real glamour, and *The Death of Fionavar* might take its place beside the *Deirdre* of AE and the *Deirdre* of Synge for its enchantment. Beautiful as are the complete poems with which the book begins and ends, there are passages of the play that have the poppy and mandragora of poetic vision and sweet music. There is a lovely bit in which 'A Warrior' tells how Fionavar died:

*She came at evening running to the field,*
*Knowing naught of battle nor sights that appal*
*The strongest soul unused to the ways of war.*
*Thou knowest her heart was ever wont to burn*
*For any little grief. Therefore when she saw*
*The primroses soaked in blood and the brown fern*
*Broken; Death that was servant to no gentle god;*
*And everywhere pale faces wild with pain,*
*The blood-stained daisy cried out from the sod*
*Unto her soul; there on the stricken plain*
*For very pity she fell down and died.*

The volume of TM Kettle's *Poems and Parodies* is too inclusive, but perhaps it had to be inclusive to make a volume. This brilliant young Irishman had not made a business nor a profession of poetry. He arrived at its achievement with the last few years of his short life; and none can doubt that his generous death on the battlefield was the finest poem he ever made. Much of the contents of this book are verses *á servir*. One is tolerably certain that he himself would not have included them; but reading his best one realizes what Ireland and literature have lost. He was not playing at poetry. He was writing with his heart's blood when he made the two perfect sonnets with which the book opens. Somehow they seem too personal for quotation. Kettle was much loved and much admired. It was one of life's ironies that England should have deplored premature death; not literary England, for that would have been right, but the England for whose cause it was presumed that he fell.

He had, when he chose, an extraordinary deftness in poetry, especially in an arbitrary metre like the sonnets; those two beautiful sonnets arrive at the climax with all the deft certainty of the Elizabethans; and the like is true of his 'Ballade Autumnal', which Francois Villon might have turned. His imitations, or adaptations, of Kipling are so good that one grudges them. One is happier when he answers Kipling 'Giving back his scorn' in the fine passion of 'Ulster'. In the Parnell poems he forgets altogether the air of the Tragic Jester which is in so much of his best poetry. I discovered for myself in the *Irish Review*, soon after returning to Ireland, the poem which appears here as 'Asquith in Dublin', and was greatly impressed by its fierce and passionate loyalty, which I shared. It was signed there 'Bricriu', which I understand is 'The Bitter Tongue'. It was bitter – and sweet – to the great dead:

> *You stepped your steps and the music marched and the torches tossed,*
> *As you filled your streets with your comic Pentecost,*
> *And the little English went by and the lights grew dim;*
> *We, dumb in the shouting crowd, we thought of him.*
>
> *Of him, too great for us and our souls and ways;*
> *Too great for laughter or love, praise or dispraise;*
> *Of him and the wintry swords and the closing gloom –*
> *Of him going forth alone to his lonely doom.*
> *No shouts, my Dublin, then. Not a light nor a cry!*
> *You kept them all till now when the little English go by!*

I have only one objection to make to this poem. Dublin was true to Parnell. But alas, alas, alas, that all this brilliance should have gone out on the fields of France, and that we shall have no more books from Tom Kettle.

These four books I have named are all influenced by events in Ireland of today and yesterday. I turn now to some books hardly so influenced. Lady Gilbert's beautiful poetry derives much of its inspiration from her love of Ireland: but in her enclosed garden of poetry the clamour and the cries of battle are not heard. 'Our Lady of the Irish Hills'; 'The Irish Franciscan'; 'Corcomroe'; such poetry is full of the story of Ireland and her tragic destinies, and the love of her own people is in the many ballad poems of Ireland. Sometimes there is a more fiery strain as in 'Glenmalure', written, one feels sure, in that prosperous time when Ireland was casting away the things of the spirit for material things as fast as ever she could. But somehow one thinks of Lady Gilbert's poetry as the poetry of peace and love and the Religion, and to be sure these may well be in the poetry of Ireland. Here is a jewelled song in which her lovely gift finds full expression:

> Come into the house, sweetheart,
>   Built for me and thee;
> With a lover's mystic art,
>   Dwell in it with me.

> We've a rainbow for a roof,
>   Windows framed in gold,
> Curtains of a silver woof,
>   With red roses in their fold,
> Glimmering on walls that are
>   Old as the morning star.

> See, the flooring for thy feet
>   Lilies overstrew,
> And thy couch of meadowsweet
>   Fragrant is with dew.

*There's a water-mirror smooth*
*For thy rose-face to look in,*
*There's a thrush's song to soothe,*
*A moon-wheel thy dreams to spin.*
*Here's thy gown of saffron silk,*
*And thy kirtle white as milk.*

*I've dew diamonds for thy hair,*
*Ring to fit thy hand.*
*We will travel with feet bare*
*Through the fairy land.*
*With the rain upon our brows*
*And the sunshine in our eyes,*
*We will live within the house God*
*has builded for the wise.*
*Giving endless length of lease*
*In eternal peace.*

Lady Gilbert's volume might bear the superscription:

*Fair Quiet, have I found thee here,*
*And Innocence, thy sister dear?*

Miss Letts is rather Irish by adoption and natural love, one feels, than by birth. But she loves Ireland, if not more than the Irish, at least as well. Her poetry reveals a very sweet and bountiful nature: the victims – or victors – of the war, the poor of God, the Little Brethren: she has many compassions. Her *Hallowe'en and Poems of the War* is a book of gentleness, quiet, beauty. Here is a poem which has the spirit of Herbert and something of his vision:

# ANGELIC SERVICE

No angel is so high
But serveth clowns and kings
And doeth lowly things:
He in His serviceable love can see
The symbol of some heavenly mystery
So, common things grow wings.

No angel bravely dressed
In larkspur-coloured gown,
But he will bend him down
And sweep with careful art the meanest floor.
Singing the while he sweeps and toiling more
Because he wears a crown.

Set water on to boil,
An angel helps thee straight;
Kneeling beside the grate,
With pursed mouth he bloweth up the flame,
Chiding the tardy kettle that for shame
Would make an angel wait.

And that same toil-worn broom,
So humble in thine eyes,
Perchance hath donned disguise,
And is a seraph on this errand bent,
To show thee service is a sacrament,
And Love wears servant's guise.

Louis McQuilland is a pleasant name to the Irish who read that good friend of Ireland the *New Witness*, which is manned by good knights in the service of God and the Right. The poetry of *A Song of the Open Road* is mainly bookish and urbane, such as may be written by a man who knows the fascination of London town and the ways of bookmen living and dead – for there are many ghostly men of letters who haunt the purlieus of Fleet Street and The Strand.

It is very deft and somewhat artificial, the verse essays of the Roaring '90s, rather than anything more immediate. But if his ballades and dead ladies are *vieux jeux* and rightly artificial, a sincerity which overleaps the formal measure is kept for the Country the Young.

*There is a kingdom cool and green,*
*Washed by the ever-moaning sea,*
*From whose wild surf, with furious mien,*
*Lir's bloodhounds struggle to be free.*
*The tempest breaks on tower and tree,*
*Exultingly proud winds are flung*
*Joy in the storm the watchers see*
*It is the country of the young.*

*There is a land that loved the green*
*Through all the sullen, bitter years,*
*The vengeance of the Tudor Queen,*
*Swart Cromwell's wrath,*
*proud Strafford's fears;*
*The Boyne's despair and Limerick's tears;*
*They fade, they die, as tunes long sung.*
*Youth springs triumphant down the years.*

*It is the country of the young.*
*There is a land where hope is green,*
*Exultant in the eastern sky*
*Flashes a dawn whose golden sheen*
*Shall fall where Tone and Emmet lie.*
*The brave hearts sleep, they cannot die.*
*They speak to all with deathless tongue,*
*Who serve the Cause with purpose high*
*Within the country of the young.*

## L'ENVOI

*Fair is your crown, Dark Rosaleen,*
*For you are silver joy-bells swung;*
*A nation comes to hail you Queen,*
*All in the country of the young.*

The cover design of *Little White Roads* is a heart within which is an unmistakably Irish valley with a little road meandering through it between little hills, the little hills and valleys which, like the psalmists, praise the Lord. It is symbolical of the love of Ireland in the poet's heart. This young poet has not yet quite found his way to his real gift. He is still obsessed with his reading and his admirations. But Ireland teaches, and one of those days he will find simple, sincere, and passionate expression of what comes now in but occasional felicities, of which this is one:

*If you go out in Erin when the moon is silver-bright*
*And the creeping twilight shadows cast a glimmering fairy light,*
*You will see a phantom army trooping through the fields of night*
*On the road to royal Tara.*

*The Wild Geese of a thousand fields have flown across the sea*
*From their ravaged graves in Flanders by the Yser and the Lys,*
*And they tread the plains of Erin to renew their fealty*
*To the Queen who reigns in Tara.*

*Like snowflakes in the sunshine the army melts away,*
*On a spreading tide of crimson comes the blushing dawn of day,*
*But their sleep will be uneasy in their beds of hallowed clay*
*Till the harp resounds in Tara.*

These are an autumn's Irish poets, and not all are here. There is not one who, in his or her degree, has not achievement.

*Studies: an Irish Quarterly Review,*
Vol. 6, No. 22, June 1917

# JOINING THE COLOURS ✠ *Katharine Tynan*

There they go marching all in step so gay!
Smooth-cheeked and golden, food for shells and guns.
Blithely they go as to a wedding day,
The mothers' sons.

The drab street stares to see them row on row
On the high tram-tops, singing like the lark.
Too careless-gay for courage, singing they go
Into the dark.

With tin whistles, mouth-organs, any noise,
They pipe the way to glory and the grave;
Foolish and young, the gay and golden boys
Love cannot save.

High heart! High courage! The poor girls they kissed
Run with them: they shall kiss no more, alas!
Out of the mist they stepped-into the mist
Singing they pass.

*Westminster Gazette*, 1914

**MIGRATION** ❇ *Bernard O'Donoghue*

Ledwidge was busy the day before he died,
building a lakeside road like the back road
along the Boyne to Swynnerton from Slane.

The fowler came at break of day, and took him
from his song. The words in his head as he worked –
merle or ouzel or *lon dubh* – exploded in him.
He could not stand aside while others fought
to guard old Ireland's freedom. So he said.

There was no fence or gatepost by that road
to which he could have pinned whatever lines
might cross his mind before the short night came.

Our compliment of native blackbirds
are reinforced in winter by battalions
that fly down the North Sea and Baltic
to escape the cold and then join up
with the first February chorus of the spring.

from *The Seasons of Cullen Church* (Faber, 2016)

# BY A PLACE AND A TIME

## Con Houlihan

THE FARM labourers are no longer an endangered species – they are extinct. There are still farm workers – but the farm labourer in all his glory is no more. 'Glory' may seem a wildly irrelevant word to use in such a context – but it is not.

The good farm labourer – and the profession had little room for bad ones – knew glory, even though it was not of the kind that comes with headlines and cheering crowds. He experienced it in the inner glow that comes from work well done – even though that work may have been poorly remunerated and carried out in conditions that could be a lot better.

And just as a stable lad might look at a horse as more truly belonging to him that to the owner, so too a farm labourer could regard the fields he worked as in a way his own. It was his spiritual reward – and indeed he had little else; in general, they were an abused class.

The history of the word *spailpín* is indicative: once it denoted a reaper who travelled around following the harvest; today, in those places where English is still speckled with Gaelic, it signifies a worthless fellow. The change the word had suffered is a remarkable tribute to the Irish caste system – because the *spailpín*, the farm labourer turned specialist for the harvest, was a man of great value.

There is no need to lapse into sentimentality so that he may appear in a good light – the facts are compelling. The typical farm labourer could, for instance, mow half an Irish acre of hay in a day. That area is almost four thousand square yards – think about it the next time you are sweating over your lawn. And he had to know what to do if a horse got the colic or if a cow had difficulty in calving. He had in short to be endowed with many skills and varied wisdom – and great hardihood.

And yet you will find little about him in the recorded history of this country. Indeed, if you wish for glimpses into his life you must look elsewhere – at, for example, the mowing of the great meadow in *Anna Karenina* and various scenes in Thomas Hardy. But there were two Irish farm labourers about whose lives we know a little: one, Owen Roe O'Sullivan, was a poet – the other, Patrick Ledwidge, was the father of one.

Owen Roe's life has been the subject of outrageous romanticism: like Robert Burns he survives in the folk memory as a great rake and a prodigious poet and wit and scholar. The facts of Burns's life are easily verified: he was a tortured, craven man – and his early death was brought on by working in the cold and the wet.

O'Sullivan's life is shadowier: he was probably a teacher in winter and a farm labourer for the rest of the year. He spent a while in the British Navy – and died sordidly enough after a fight in a Killarney pub that left him with a head wound that bad nursing compounded.

Patrick Ledwidge had a least two things in common with Burns and O'Sullivan: he died young – and he did not allow the heavy labour of the fields to cripple his spirit. Poetry had been their anodyne: his was the ambition that his children would get a better start in the world than he did.

Francis Ledwidge, in a letter to an American professor, wrote: 'I am of a family who were ever soldiers and poets ... I have heard my mother say many times that the Ledwidges were once a great people in the land ... ' In that touching belief he and she showed themselves to be part of the great Irish dream of their day.

Patrick Ledwidge may indeed have been a member of a family that, like Tess Durbeyfield's, had come down in the world – but whatever the case, he was a migrant labourer when he married Anne Lynch in Slane in 1872. They settled in a two-roomed cottage – and he worked on a farm where, between wages and extras such as milk and fuel, he earned about fifteen shillings a week.

It sounds miserably small – but it was well above the average for the time: you should bear in mind that in the 1940s few farm labourers made thirty shillings a week. Obviously, Patrick was an exceptional worker, and his wife shared his ambitions for their children. They soon got a cottage from the Rural District Council, at Janeville, about a quarter of a mile from Slane.

It was a spacious little house – you can still see it – and with it was a half-acre of good land. The Ledwidges' plans were coming on nicely. Patrick, the eldest son, stayed on as a monitor in his national school – the dream was under way.

To read now about Patrick and Anne and their young family is to go back to an age of epic innocence. It was a time of hope, compounded of many elements – including Victorian self-improvement, Irish nationalism, and the general intuition that the world was improving. The land war was being won and the dispossessed were confident that they would come back into their little kingdoms.

But the Ledwidges' ladder was shatteringly pulled from beneath them – Patrick died suddenly. Anne was left with eight children, the youngest only three months old. It was the kind of tragedy that makes the light of Shakespeare's protagonists seem self-imposed.

The only state assistance then was a shilling a week for every child, but Anne did not put any of her family into the home.

She was determined to keep them together, and so this Mother Courage went into the fields to earn what she could by weeding and thinning and snagging and picking. And when there was little work on the land, she knitted and washed and darned. The work in the fields was paid by piece rate, and her prowess was the wonder of the locality.

Patrick had to abandon his hopes of going on to be a teacher; he stayed on at school until he learned book-keeping and got a job in Dublin. Now he became the family bread earner. But he was soon back home, afflicted with the scourge of the time – tuberculosis. The young people of today do not know the terrible effects of that disease. Once the sufferer discovered he had it, he resigned himself to death – and if, as was usually the case, he remained at home, the family were to some extent ostracised.

Patrick lingered on in the cottage near Slane for four years; his mother was again back working in the fields. One day she faced up to the final humiliation: she could not pay the rent – and the bailiff and the police came to evict the family. The local doctor intervened and certified that Patrick could not be moved.

His death brought further humiliation – he was buried 'on the parish'. Francis later wrote of the years when it seemed 'as though God had forgotten us'.

There is a strange parallel between the life of the Ledwidges and that of DH Lawrence's family. You will remember how Lawrence's mother was determined that her eldest son would not go down into the mines, and kept him at school until he got a job as a clerk in London. He too was soon dead – and the Lawrences knew the dreadful feeling that comes when you believe that fate has turned against you.

Anne Ledwidge seemingly believed that God moved in very mysterious ways – at any rate Francis never heard her complain. She was free from the worst of all Irish diseases – self-pity. The dream, though tattered, went on. The children were kept at school until they could find reasonable places in the world.

Francis left school after his Confirmation. He was almost fourteen – it was not uncommon then for lads of ten to be full-time labourers in the fields. Young Ledwidge became an apprentice cook at Slane Castle but his stay was short – his sense of humour undid him. One morning he rubbed out the day's menu on the kitchen slate and substituted such delicacies as spuds and bacon and cabbage. The cook was not amused.

He next tried the grocery trade and spent three whole days in a shop in Rathfarnham. Then he stole away in the night and walked the thirty miles back to Slane. Although he was not fully aware of it then, he had made the momentous decision: he had declared himself a poet.

Since childhood he had been uttering and scribbling verses – and in his Dublin exile had suddenly felt that poetry was his vocation. And he sensed too a truth that a great Greek poet Cavafy was later to express: 'In those few streets or fields where you grew up, there you will live and there you will die.'

Back at home he got a job as gardener-cum-yard boy with a liberal young couple who treated him in a civilised manner and paid him far above the average wage. After three years they left for Dublin, and Francis, now twenty, went to work as a road mender with the County Council.

In between jobs he had often worked in the fields and, in his fumbling way, was becoming well-equipped to understand his heartland. It is often said that his poetry is too literary, that he wrote out of *The Golden Treasury* rather than out of life. But that is not true at all – and those who say so do not know Meath, that county of rich land and noble trees and a great sense that nature is bountiful.

And if the stony grey soil of Monaghan burgled Patrick Kavanagh's bank of youth, so did the essence of Meath affect Francis Ledwidge. There was another great difference between them: they grew up in eras that, though separated by only a generation, seem centuries apart. Ledwidge's Ireland was full of yeast: *Ulysses* is a brilliant book but it performed a post mortem on a body that was about to waken from a deep slumber.

Ledwidge grew up in an atmosphere of hope that now seems pathetically naïve but that was, in fact, sensible and wholesome. He studied the Gaelic language in his spare time; he played the new code of football; he was a vigorous worker in the budding labour movement.

Kavanagh's Ireland gave out a sour smell like an abandoned porter jar. He grew up in an atmosphere of economic depression and spiritual sickness. The sickness came from a sense of betrayal: 'native government' (was it ever really such?) had not brought the promised land.

The miracle of Kavanagh is that he sang so well in such a place and time. And if there is a softness in Francis Ledwidge it comes from two things. He lived in a world of an innocence we have lost forever, and his poetry was written in youth. He went across the river and into the trees at thirty.

Tributaries, *Evening Press*, 29 July 1980

*Jessica Traynor*

WHEN I was in secondary school I loved history. I think it appealed because it tested both memory and creativity – can you remember all the facts, and can you order them in a way that tells a story? However, the sheer volume of facts and figures became hard to bear as my Leaving Cert drew near. The addition of a 'special topic', a module of self-guided study and research, felt like the straw that might break the camel's back.

My teacher took me aside and brought my attention to Francis Ledwidge. She had insight enough to know that the juxtaposition of literature and history would appeal. I went and purchased *Francis Ledwidge: A Life of the Poet* by Alice Curtayne, and became immersed in Ledwidge's story; in his early life and loves, his interactions with Lord Dunsany and the cosmopolitan literary world of Dublin, the beautiful poems he sent home from the Front, and his tragic end at the Battle of Passchendaele.

Ledwidge was my introduction to the kind of study where the writer is asked to form their own opinions, rather than simply learning them by rote. I found freedom in poignant poems that range from the fertile fields of Meath to the battlefields of Flanders.

Dublin, March 2017

# NOCTURNE ✺ *Jessica Traynor*


I remember the poppy –
the poppy you still see everywhere,
but there were none in the war,

only mud and tunnels making cities
and men in them digging in the dark,
shells screaming in the earth.

✺

They wanted me
to go back,
see the graves
like little matchsticks.
I couldn't.

✺

Sometimes in the night
I think of them – the lads
all waking in the dark
with no one to talk to them at all.

And if I was to go there,
I wouldn't know what to say
and I couldn't bear to leave them
when the night came.

## MORSE ✠ *Jessica Traynor*

He taps teaspoon on mug,
wipes crumbs into
the palm of his hand.
*dot, dot, dot, dash –*

but the radio posts
are all closed now,
gone like the long-wave
that swept its arc

through the night-time sky
sending whispers to corners
where thoughts
lay waiting to be caught.

He thinks a falling away
has occurred, the kind
that drops the scales
from the world's eyes

and loses the world in the process;
and though no one is listening,
morse for him is everywhere,
a second heartbeat

thrumming the morning;
the click of his bicycle spokes
the faint but certain patter
of applause from the TV,

the fractious beeping
of car alarms. All messages
shouted into the world –
lost. He tries not to listen,

as once during an episode
he tried to stop counting
his footsteps. But on
an April morning

at the bus stop,
umbrella unfurled,
spring rain on the canvas –
the memory of kisses,

the crackle of a drowned fire
somehow still burning –
makes the last man
at the last listening post
                                        smile.

# NIMRUD   ❈   *Jessica Traynor*


When recovering in hospital
the steroids conjured the radio's

talk of beheadings in Nimrud
to a dirge in your ear,

till the words you learned
as a child poured from you:

*The Assyrian came down like a wolf on the fold ...*
Byron's rhythms beating drums in your veins.

You were never one to remember a poem,
but in that ward it infected you –

we tried to laugh the possession away,
as the radio sang of black-clad men

blasting their marks on ruins,
pulling wings from the sphinx,

slashing its sightless eyes,
only to succeed in redacting themselves –

much as the words of the poem
fell away from you when we took you home.

# AMONG THE DOLOROUS
# AND LOVELY

## Tom French

*Who enters age amenably?*
*Who but a lucky few*
*complete their lives? ...*

'A Family Tie', **PETER FALLON**
from *Strong, My Love* (The Gallery Press, 2014)

*'In summary, Third Ypres*
*was a wasteful failure ...'*

*1914–1918 The History of the First World War,*
**DAVID STEVENSON** (Penguin Books, 2005)

SEPTEMBER 2013. I'm driving out of Navan, past Blackcastle, Dunmoe, Donaghmore (and Matty & Winnie McGoona's house which is no longer there), heading east to Slane to meet a man who knows the lay of the land. He is a fisherman descended from poachers who could, he says, catch a buck hare out in the middle of a green field. On one of his recent visits to the County Archive we looked at the pages at the back of the Slane Mill accounts book which are headed *Slane Colliery 1773*. William Burton Conyngham and his fellow investors sank £25 each into opening a shaft in July of that year, followed by a second in the early autumn. My guide remembers cattle sheltering from the wind in the late 1940s in the hollows which those excavations of the early 1770s left.

I pass through Beauparc. In September 1917 the Dublin Industrial Development Association requested particulars as to why the Beauparc Copper Mines had been closed and when they had last been working. Copper for munitions work was in short supply and the British government was importing copper from Spain and Canada. Mr Owens, mine owner and mineralogist, reported that a shaft had been sunk to a depth of 140 feet, and a seam 3 feet thick of pure ore had been discovered and worked. He reported that the machinery was not good enough to extract the copper, and that the shareholders were unwilling to subscribe the necessary additional capital.

Only the week previous, a former Beauparc miner had found himself in the wrong place at the wrong time in Belgium and had been blown to pieces by a German shell. Had he lived he might have lived to hear shells containing Beauparc ore sailing over his head into enemy lines.

❊    ❊    ❊

I HAVE been trying to write a poem about a photograph of a handful of Seaforth Highlanders – Canadians of Scottish descent – in a potato field on the road from Amiens to Albert, helping with the harvest in October 1916. So far, it goes:

> *The Seaforth Highlanders have paused to help*
> *    a farmer on the road from Amiens to Albert.*
> *It is tatie hoking time. They can't resist*
> *    throwing off their packs and stacking rifles*

*to postpone death by bending astride drills*
*            and bearing the ache in hamstrings and backs*
*as they handle the turned earth and caress*
*            a handful of the yield one hand digs up*

*while the other digs in to turn up more.*
*            There's talk of them tasting like balls of flour.*
*Mucking in here makes it peace time briefly.*

*The scent of potatoes brings back the bothy,*
*            straw mattresses arrayed on seed boxes,*
*the cow house swept out for men to lie down.*

*Amiens-Albert, October 1916*

All that winter, in France and Flanders, the weather would be making the news, the temperature staying below freezing for nearly three months. In that 'tide of khaki flowing out of Folkestone Harbour across the Channel', as Alice Curtayne writes, the poet was destined for Picquigny, a village north-east of Amiens. Katharine Tynan, whose sons were also serving, wrote to Ledwidge there. In his reply, dated 6 January 1917, he wrote:

> *If I survive the war, I have great hopes of writing something that will live. If not, I trust to be remembered in my own land for one or two things which its long sorrow inspired. My book has had a greater reception in England, Ireland and America than I had ever dreamt of, but I never feel that my name should be mentioned in the same breath with my contemporaries.*
>
> *You ask me what I am doing. I am a unit in the Great War, doing and suffering, admiring great endeavour and condemning great dishonour. I may be dead before this reaches you, but I will have done my part. Death is as interesting to me as life.*

*I have seen so much of it from Suvla to Serbia, and now in France. I am always homesick. I hear the roads calling, and the hills, and the rivers wondering where I am. It is terrible to be always homesick.*

In *The Years of the Shadow* she wrote of him:

*At that picture show of AE's ... I added a new acquaintance – rather two new acquaintances – in Lord Dunsany, and Francis Ledwidge who was going round the pictures very much under the wing of Lord Dunsany ... Ledwidge was wrapped up in a huge frieze coat. It gave one the impression somehow of covering a multitude of sins. His face, as I remember it, had no likeness to the nimimy-piminy Bunthorne picture of him which appeared in some papers after his death, nor to the private soldier one I have seen in a Christmas number of The Bookman. I carried away an impression of a newly washed, red-and-white wholesomeness. One felt he ought to have been very fair if the sun had not ruddied and goldened him.*

Approaching the village of Slane, I drive past potato fields. Signs tell you that you are entering 'Ledwidge Country'. If you haven't heard the name before, the signs mean nothing. If you have, you start to pay attention. I have stared at the space between the entries 'Ledward, Patricia' and 'Lee, Joseph' in the index to *The Oxford Handbook of British & Irish War Poetry* and failed to see the words 'Ledwidge, Francis' because they do not occur. Ledwidge is almost the perfect opposite of the description Michael Longley gives of himself in his introduction to *Cenotaph of Snow: Sixty Poems about War*, as 'a non-combatant drawn to the subject of war'. Ledwidge is our combatant *sui generis*, our enigma consumed in a wasteful failure, destined neither to enter age nor to complete his life, who was drawn to the subject of home.

A couple of doors down from The Conyngham Arms in Slane, the name and the year 'Nat Miles A.D. 1769' are engraved on a stone between two second-storey windows. That name, though remote in time, rings a bell. Amongst the piggin staves and winch handles and scantling purchased to construct the mine shaft, there are the expenses incurred to wake and bury one Valentine Read, a child labourer who died, it seems, as a result of a cave-in. Nat Miles's name appears in the colliery accounts as the vendor of shrouding purchased to wrap the boy's body.

The excavations of that summer of 1773 are remembered in the name of the townland – *Coalpits* – as recorded by the Ordnance Survey of Ireland, and in the phrase which appears on the 6" map of 1837 – *Shaft sunk in search of coal.* On this high ground, up behind the Little Wood, we can see nearly all the way to the coast. The sun today is splitting the stones. At the gate into the field we stop at a tin-roofed, mud-walled cottage, which has been encroached upon by young ash, and is not far off becoming a ruin. A tiny pane of glass is set into the side wall of the fireplace facing the front door. My guide says, 'I have it to say I drank tea in this house.'

On the page where news of Ledwidge's death appeared in the *Meath Chronicle* of 4 August 1917, life went on as before – a goat trespassed on cabbages and potatoes, someone was drunk and disorderly; total daily war expenditure of the belligerent nations was estimated at £50,000,000; children were neglected by their labouring father, a farmer was fined for failing to dip his sheep; the Reichstag passed the third reading of the war credit of 750,000,000 Deutschmarks with only the Independent Socialists voting against it; a Kilcock tenant was reinstated; a milk contractor refused to sign a bond; Fr. O'Farrell PP wrote to congratulate the Kells Choir for their singing at Kieran Well on the first Sunday in August (where the sacred trout appears, makes the sign of the cross and disappears again until the following year), and Navan Urban District Council debated long into the night the cost of gas for lighting the town.

Darkness was being banished from the towns of Meath. No. I cannot say that Darkness was being *contravened*. The dog days of August had come and Lady Day was approaching. Pilgrims suffering with eye complaints would be making the journey to Slane to walk to the well in the hopes of a cure.

A crop of oats has been harvested in the past few weeks. The contours of the stubbled ground are easy to see, and no hollows are visible now. Young Valentine Read is immortalised in the accounts, but it is an unlovely memorial. I imagine the shock wave of bad news travelling up and out from the coal shaft, into the village of Slane where it breaks on his mother's ears – '... killed at once ... he suffered no pain ...' – her hands flying to her face; that part of herself – his body – being winched back up to the surface to be washed and rubbed with oils and wrapped in shrouding; and his last wages – the 10s. 8d. – being left on the table for her when she'll be able to look at it, to touch it, without retching.

*Valentine Read, for the difference there is*
*between sinking a shaft through shale for coal*
*and sinking a grave, here, accounted let your life be.*

*Among pick helves, piggin staves, turn tree,*
*1s. 1d. for the trip to Trim to bring the coroner;*
*among winch handles, scantling, superficial timber,*

*to Nat Miles for five yards of shrouding 5s. 5d.;*
*for camber oak, hoops for the whim shaft, spikes,*
*to Thomas North for nails, for tobacco and pipes*

*5s. 5d., 'oyl for the whim' 2s. 8d.; for strong spirits*
*to rub your broken body, and brandy for drinking*
*2s. 81/2d.; ale for the men repairing the shaft on Sunday*

*2s. 4d; for the labour of your last eight days*
*on earth (at 1s. 8d. a day), 10s. 8d. This account*
*being settled in full, go, child, into eternity.*

*Slane Colliery, September 1773*

There is another crop, of family names from Slane and district, listed in A.J. Horneck's *County Meath Roll of Honour*, that starts with 'Conyngham' and ends with 'Thunder' and includes Flood, Lynch, Vaughey, Murphy, Owens, Connolly, Govern, Lane, Carolan, Ledwidge, Mongey, Gillic, Fitzpatrick, Clarke, Kinsella, McGuirk, Healy, Reilly, Gorman, Feeley, Duffy. He is one among many. Slane has been generous with its young. He is one of a kind.

In the 'Introductory' Horneck writes:

*Many, very many, have been disabled for life,*
*and many families in Meath have had*
*the horrors of this titanic War brought home*
*to them by the loss of some beloved member.*
*In placing on record the names of the Brave*
*Men of Meath who have so unselfishly*
*answered the Nation's Call, we feel that we*
*shall to some extent be instrumental*
*in alleviating the anguish in many an humble home;*
*and further, in compiling these lists, we realise*
*we are only paying a worthy tribute to the men*
*who have so nobly taken upon themselves the national duty*
*of upholding the traditional bravery of the Irish race,*
*and of vindicating the honour of their country.*

The lines scan. Horneck has almost inadvertently written a sonnet about Meath and the war, which reads like a citation and which reminds me, in turn, of Michael Longley's sonnet 'Citation':

*It is like a poem. It is better than a poem,*
*the citation for my father's Military Cross*
*dividing itself up into lines like this: 'For*
*conspicuous gallantry and devotion to duty ...*

'Duty', 'bravery', 'country' – the rhymes in Horneck's paragraph are heaped against the unsuspecting. Poetry is being employed in the recruitment drive. The collective noun for 'young men' in the county – and in Ireland – at the time is 'a substantial reserve'. They are spoken of in the language used to speak of coal and ore, of minerals to be mined from the earth and to be returned to it.

❉   ❉   ❉

Truth be told, I had no business trying to write anything. My people, on both sides, were tending their animals and saving crops when the nations of the earth were discovering that it was possible to shell each other into oblivion. I had no business trying to write anything that might have anything to do with the Great War. I had no intention of writing a poem at all. It was oblivion that got me started, and that kept me going. It was *that* war which kept suggesting itself.

My wife's father served with the London Rifles (x Corps) in North Africa during the Second World War. A wallet survives bearing, in his handwriting, the place names *Tabarka, Bizerte, Tebourba, Mateur, Hamam Lif, Naples*. Bob was a cog in the wheel of Operation Torch, which began on 8 November 1942, four days after Rommel began his long withdrawal. The ultimate objectives were the Tunisian port and airfield complex of Bizerte and the capital city of Tunis. Command of those facilities would allow the Allies to bomb Sicily, protect the Malta convoys, and strike at Rommel's supply lines.

The biggest experience of Bob's youth was hardly spoken of. The British lost 200,000 men in the North Africa campaign. His service record locates him at the POW camp at Mateur for ten days where the Germans were succumbing in their thousands to typhoid. I tell my children that they would not be here had Bob not managed to come home in one piece. They look at me. (My first born recently recited 'dulce et decorum est pro patria mori' to me, and the experience of hearing it from his mouth has stayed with me). In a couple of years he will be old enough to lie about his age and enlist. They are young enough still to be unable to imagine a time when I won't be here.

Bob's brother Jim was trained in commando tactics and dropped behind enemy lines in Burma with the Chindits (named after the symbolic guardian of Burmese temples, a mythical beast, half lion, half-flying griffin). A snapshot survives of him at home in his aviary in Alperton. He is hardly more than a boy. Their father before them served with the Royal Field Artillery and made it home too. A brother-in-law was never right after. He'd been assigned to cleaning out flying fortresses when they returned from bombing missions. What he saw unsettled him for the rest of his life.

It was looking at photographs and moving images in news bulletins that drew me in. In January 1998 Japanese Prime Minister Ryutaro Hashimoto apologised to Britain and increased the amount spent on exchange visits to Japan for the grandchildren of British PoWs. But his apology failed to satisfy many British PoWs who insisted he use a key Japanese word *shazai*. The word 謝罪 (*shazai*) is composed of 謝 *sha*, 'to apologize/thank/refuse' and 罪

*zai*, 'guilt/crime/fault.' Hearing that one word from the lips of the
Japanese Prime Minister would have meant the world.

In May of the same year Emperor Akihito and Empress Michiko
arrived in Britain on a state visit. The surviving servicemen, feeling
betrayed, attended in dress uniform and, as their Queen and the
Emperor passed in an open carriage through the streets of the
capital, turned their backs in exact, parade ground fashion.

> *When the grandfathers and shell-shocked bachelors*
> *pinned fluttering ribbon and medals to their chests*
> *and gathered to watch the Emperor of Japan pass,*
> *word passed through the ranks to turn their backs,*
> *a parade ground exercise they executed perfectly*
> *because they had performed it perfectly for real.*
>
> *Turning as one at the signal on a single heel*
> *they faced again into the crosshairs of Canons*
> *and saluted, as they had their own hall mirrors,*
> *the faces of men they remembered in the throng,*
> *linked arms, and held the line, and did not flinch*
> *though some were weeping, others consoling them.*

They turned their back on their queen who had turned her
back on them. And it broke their hearts.

Then there was the photograph in a weekend supplement,
the caption to which read 'The Habsburg uniforms of 1914 were
meticulously differentiated between ten shades of red'; the story
Seamus Smyth tells of 'Snow' Gough who survived the war and
delivered coal in Navan for years – 'Snow, did you ever kill a
man?' and 'Snow's 'Every night I close my eyes I see them'; then
the four clips from the original footage shot at the Somme and a
sentence in the narrative which said '*The Battle of the Somme* was

the only war footage in the history of British social cinema to be screened uncensored; intended to raise morale, it had the opposite effect.' One person in the throng in the cinema in Leicester Square points at the screen and calls out, 'My God. He's been shot.' And a whole cinema full of people tries to get a look at his face, to establish who he is, who he was, as he breathes his last before their very eyes.

There and then, we enter the age of war as spectacle, of Mutually Assured Destruction, the War on Terror, Black Ops, cyber-terrorism, the unmanned drone.

❉   ❉   ❉

It is early April 2014. I'm heading for Slane again, this time to Janeville. A Welsh delegation from Snowdonia National Park, including the poet Myrddin ap Dafydd, are visiting the Ledwidge Museum. In March 2012 the Snowdonia National Park Authority announced that it had purchased for the nation, with the support of the Welsh Government and the National Heritage Memorial Fund, Yr Ysgwrn, the 18th Century farmhouse in Trawsfynydd which was the home of the chair-winning poet Hedd Wyn.

His name in English was Ellis Humphrey Evans, the poet-shepherd who enlisted in the 15th Battalion of the Royal Welsh Fusiliers at the turn of 1917 and was killed on the first day of the Battle of Passchendaele on 31 July 1917. Ledwidge and Hedd Wyn – like Pablo Neruda and W.H. Auden – died on the same day. The figures overwhelm – 100,000 British troops, eighteen square miles of territory, 27,000 casualties – almost the current entire population of the town of Navan; 135,000 killed in one sector for a gain of one hundred yards, the distance from the back door at Janeville to the back garden wall.

It was a nosecap shell to the stomach that killed Hedd Wyn. At the first-aid post, it is recorded that he asked the doctor treating him, 'Do you think that I will live?' Even then, in extremis, one imagines what was in the back of his mind was all that he would not now be granted time to write. Six weeks later, at Birkenhead, when it was announced that Hedd Wyn was the winner of the Eisteddfod, the chair was draped in black cloth. It has been known since as The Black Chair. Visitors flock to look at it, but nobody will ever sit in it again.

His most quoted poem 'War' must sound, as I can only imagine it in the original Welsh, like a spell –

> *Gwae fi fy myw mewn oes mor ddreng,*
> *A Duw ar drai ar orwel pell;*
> *O'i ôl mae dyn, yn deyrn a gwreng,*
> *Yn codi ei awdurdod hell.*

> *Pan deimlodd fyned ymaith Dduw*
> *Cyfododd gledd i ladd ei frawd;*
> *Mae sŵn yr ymladd ar ein clyw,*
> *A'i gysgod ar fythynnod tlawd.*

> *Mae'r hen delynau genid gynt,*
> *Ynghrog ar gangau'r helyg draw,*
> *A gwaedd y bechgyn lond y gwynt,*
> *A'u gwaed yn gymysg efo'r glaw.*

> *Why must I live in this grim age,*
> *when, to a far horizon, God*
> *has ebbed away, and man, with rage,*
> *now wields the sceptre and the rod?*

*Man raised his sword, once God had gone,*
*to slay his brother, and the roar*
*of battlefields now casts upon*
*our homes the shadow of the war.*

*The harps to which we sang are hung*
*on willow boughs, and their refrain*
*drowned by the anguish of the young*
*whose blood is mingled with the rain.*

These Welsh visitors are people after our own hearts. In Janeville the fine china has been taken down from the dresser and the table laid. There are scones and jam and fresh cream. As gifts for the visitors I bring copies of *A Meath Anthology* which Meath County Council Library Service published in 2010, and my own copy of the special issue of the *Cork Review* which was published in honour of the poet Seán Dunne who also did not make old bones or complete his life.

I am taken aback to see things in Janeville that I have always known were there – the shell transformed into a miniature grotto, the books, the 'In Memoriam' in longhand in a frame on the wall, the faces of the Lace School girls in the photograph, the fiddle on the shelf. I couldn't help thinking, despite the blasphemy, of how Ledwidge's claim – and the claim of the thousands of young Irish men – on Brooke's beautiful lyric might sound:

*If I should die, think only this of me;*
*    That there's some corner of a foreign field*
*That is for ever Ireland. There shall be*
*    In that rich earth a richer dust concealed;*
*A dust whom Ireland bore, shaped, made aware,*
*    Gave, once, her flowers to love, her ways to roam,*

*A body of Ireland's breathing Irish air,*
     *Washed by the rivers, blest by suns of home.*

*And think, this heart, all evil shed away,*
     *A pulse in the eternal mind, no less*
*Gives somewhere back the thoughts by Ireland given;*
     *Her sights and sounds, dreams happy as her day;*
*And laughter, learnt of friends; and gentleness,*
     *In hearts at peace, under an Irish heaven.*

I wander up the garden behind the house and stop at the 'moss-upholstered stone' which was moved here from the farm on the Hill of Slane where Ellie Vaughey lived. Ivy is sending its tendrils across the moss.

*Bluebells swinging,*
*Shadows wildly blown,*
*A song in the wood,*
*A ship on the sea.*

He wasn't to know how love and war would meet at this stone. In the centre of John Feehan's and Grace O'Donovan's beautiful *The Bogs of Ireland* two maps face each other; the one on the left shows the centres set up for the collection of sphagnum moss by members of the Society of United Irishwomen who combed the bogs for moss during the war years; the one on the right shows the sphagnum sub-depots where the moss was manufactured into surgical dressings. Kells and Navan are marked. Because of its extraordinary absorptive capacity – twenty times its dry weight – sphagnum moss was used for staunching blood and could be left on wounds longer because it was porous and mildly antiseptic and cooled the wound. Sphagnum is not dependent on the soil for its raw materials. It gets its nutrients from the rain. A million tons were shipped to the Front. Bohermeen moss might have been used to dress his wounds.

I find a single sentence in those million tons, in which the sound of 'wounds' makes peace with the sound of 'woods', just as 'passed' and 'ash' come to be on first name terms. There is nothing to do but write it down.

> *The limbs of the injured might have passed,*
> *after the night sisters returned from the woods*
> *with baskets of moss to dress their wounds,*
> *for the limbs of beech and sycamore and ash.*
>
> *Moss (1917)*

One thinks of a convoy of ships laden with a cargo of moss, leaving the North Wall for France. It is unreasonable to think that a poem might help to make the injured whole again. And yet. Here, standing before Ellie's and Francis's trysting stone, all I know is that the poem, to begin at all, begins by being unreasonable.

⚜   ⚜   ⚜

The Isle of Man. September 2014. I am here to attend a conference on civilian internment during The Great War. The holiday makers and TT enthusiasts are all gone and we are walking the empty prom. The hundreds of men of German birth who were held in the workhouse in Oldcastle were shipped here in May 1918 to join the thousands held at Knockaloe. They marched to the boat at the North Wall to the sounds of singing and cheering, and were greeted with hat pins and slaps when they disembarked at Douglas. One woman who at first mistook the 'visitors' for Sinn Féiners was so violent in her expressions of contempt, the *Isle of Man Times* reported, that she had to be removed.

A map published in *This Terrible Ordeal: Manx Letters, Diaries and Memories of the Great War* stops me in my tracks. Crossed swords mark the theatres of major conflict throughout the world at the time. All the places you would expect are there – the Somme, Passchendaele, Gallipoli, Salonika. But, there, half an hour south of where I live, on the east coast of Ireland, where Ledwidge 'courted at the seaside/ beyond Drogheda', on this Manx map the crossed swords show Dublin as a theatre of major conflict.

The author is present to address the conference. It occurs to me I might have a word. Then it occurs to me that I might govern my tongue. The history of our Poet's Rising, of 'A noble failure is not in vain ...,' of 'He shall not hear ...' is not this history. Sons of this island, where I am a visitor, were drafted to Dublin to put the rebellion down. Sons of this island helped to make up the search parties, the gun crews, the checkpoint details, the firing squads.

We pause at the memorial on the prom to read the names of the men who died before their time. A seagull has alighted on the bronze head of the memorial soldier, and is looking toward the horizon. It puts me in mind of the prom at Portstewart where I have never been, and of *Field Work* where 'In Memoriam' first appeared, of the framed typescript on the wall in Janeville where 'papish get' appears in place of 'worried pet', of 'our dead enigma'. A seagull, a bittern, and a blackbird. Given time, their flight paths will align into four lines:

> *His forehead and temples are in clear shot,*
> *        now horizon and parapet are one and the same.*
> *The seagull that alights on his fontanel*
> *        stares out to sea for ages without moving.*

Douglas, September 2014

*     *     *

Leaving Slane that day in April, I felt grateful, not just for the hospitality. I had sat at the table and looked out at the garden through the kitchen window and remembered what Ledwidge had written to a friend, towards the end when he had had enough – 'If I heard the Germans were coming in over our garden wall, I wouldn't go out to stop them. They could come.' Looking at the stones in the wall, I could imagine two homesick Germans, one of them maybe even toting a notebook in his pocket, putting their weapons aside to help each other over it, then straightening their uniforms and great coats again to advance on the cottage, keeping an eye not to trample the snowdrops or the daffodils.

That day I fulfilled a long-held wish to read Seán Dunne's beautiful 'Francis Ledwidge's Cottage' in Francis Ledwidge's cottage. In a photograph taken that April morning, Myrddin ap Dafydd, the Welsh poet – himself twice winner of the Eisteddfod – is listening intently to the Waterford poet's words about the pilgrimage he made to the Meath poet's house. So many spirits might have been listening in.

A poem, prompted by the story of how they identified Ledwidge's remains and by a photograph in the Alice Curtayne archive box in the Meath County Archive of Ledwidge in Egypt, a notebook protruding from his tunic pocket, was still in the future. When it sees the light of day, titled 'The Thirty-First of July, Janeville', it will go:

> When they come to gather parts they will know
> his torso not by distinguishing marks but by
> the notebook tucked into the pocket of his tunic,
> and a lull before nightfall in the shelling

*will be all they will hope for to give those notes*
*and the stub of a pencil their Christian burial.*

On the road home I am reminded of what my poacher/guide said about the empty house, up behind the Little Wood, which we passed on our way to search for evidence in the landscape of coal mining. It has been used since to shelter animals and now it is on the verge of becoming a ruin, yet he remembers the conviviality of taking tea there.

I will be back this way, now that I know the road. For now, I have it to say that I leaned against the wine-coloured bricks that frame the front door and had my photo taken. I have it to say that I read Seán Dunne's poem in Francis Ledwidge's house. I have it to say that I drank tea in that house.

## THE FOURTH OF APRIL  ✠  *Tom French*


All the accoutrements of hospitality
graced a table that made scones look huge –
pristine Willow pattern depicting love,

fresh tea in a pot cozied on its stand,
jam from wayside berries in ramekins,
cream whipped in a pewter jug and transferred.

In that perfect absence of running water
I fancied I could hear a cold tap drip
as the violin kept its silence on a nail.

The only thing I could think of to say
was Seán Dunne's lovely poem about the place,
and I had in my head as I rose to leave,

a tune that needed only verses, an air –
*The Boesinghe Polka. The Winding Road to Slane.*


Janeville, 2014

# THE POET'S HOUSE   ✺   *David Wheatley*

*Where sorrel is always   about to come   into season*

*your memory   is a house where no one   lives and yet*

*among scraps of verse   pencilled on bricks   on barnyard walls*

*you return at dusk   to a rose like   a bittern's neck*

*bent over the basin   and copy them   into a jotter*

*the water poured   from your pitcher   trickling ultimately*

*into the Marne   perfidies of the moment   one last evening*

*a woodbine's flare   down the lane   a cross-cut saw's*

*chevaux de frise   saying no way back   exempla*

*of endurance   burnished by time   and unavailing*

*yet gathering   the squandered light   in your wake*

# THE YELLOW BITTERN    *David Wheatley*
## *after Cathal Buí Mac Giolla Ghunna*

My yellow bittern, a blow to me the sight
of all your bones on show, after your sport.
It wasn't the hunger did this but the drought
upending you made sure you were not spared.
Sadder to me than ever the fall of Troy
the spectacle of you laid on a bare stone,
who never harmed a soul and would not stray
from supping bog water for any wine.

Lovely bittern, heartbreak strikes me dumb
to find you on my rambles belly up,
you that I heard so many mornings boom
among the mudflats as you took a sup.
Cathal's always hearing the bitter word
from those who say he's finished, and the sauce
will kill him off, but I say, Look at this bird,
died for want of a drink, and give me peace.

Young bittern, great is my distress
at finding you among the rushes cold
and rats coming to devour all trace
of you, and the awful wake for you they'll hold.
If only you got word to me in time
about your spot of bother on the dry,
I'd have smashed the ice for the wee dram
would have brought a gleam to your dead eye.

You won't see me get carried away by baser
birds, by your blackbird, thrush or crane,
but with your hearty frolics I was sure,
bittern, that you and I were close as kin.
You never missed a chance to wet your beak
and the word round here is, I'm the same.
Any drop that's going I knock back
for fear the thirst got you might prove my doom.

My true love says if I don't ditch the booze
it's a paltry span I've left to linger,
but my answer is she's telling lies
and thanks to the drink I'll live all the longer.
Haven't you seen this thirsty bird laid low,
and it only in search of a drop of water?
Friends, the time to raise a glass is now,
for nary a sup you'll get in the hereafter.

# BIG BRITISH AIR RAIDS—21 LARGE SHIPS DOWN

# The Daily Mirror

### CERTIFIED CIRCULATION LARGER THAN THAT OF ANY OTHER DAILY PICTURE PAPER

No. 4,303. | Registered at the G.P.O. as a Newspaper | THURSDAY, AUGUST 9, 1917 | One Penny.

## HELPED TO DOWN L 48 | GUARDSMEN WITH THEIR BOOTY

Lieutenant Frank Douglas Hobler, R.F.C., who has been awarded the M.C. for his part in the destruction of L18, one of Germany's latest super-Zeppelins, in East Anglia.

### IRISH POET KILLED. | NEW WAR MINISTER.

Lce.-Cpl. Francis Ledwidge, the peasant poet of Meath, who has been killed in action in Flanders. He was twenty-six years of age.

Lieutenant-General De Ceuninck, to be Belgian War Minister vice Baron De Broqueville, now Minister for Foreign Affairs.—(Official.)

Irish Guards examining a German machine gun after the great battle of Flanders. They are seen wearing the body armour now adopted by the Huns, which also formed part of their booty. The heroism of the Irish Guards came in for special mention.—(Official photograph.)

### AFTER-CARE OF THE MAIMED SOLDIER IN GERMANY—HIGH JUMPS FOR ONE-LEGGED MEN.

Germany has opened a large establishment near Berlin for the training of men who have lost limbs in the war. Gymnastics and sports play a big part and even one-legged

men can do high jumping. Archery is a favourite pastime, while one-armed men carry out exercises with a form of Indian club

Daily Mirror, 9 August 1917
*(courtesy of the British Library)*

# A LETTER TO
# FRANCIS LEDWIDGE

*Brian Turner*

Dear Francis,

One hundred years have passed since that shell exploded and you exhaled your last breath. The world given worlds beyond counting, the human ear devising the means by which to listen to gravity itself as it rolls in waves across the landscape of time. The age of the atom, the age of information. Wave after wave of generations marching forward.

The furniture has been sold off from the houses you once knew, or they've aged into antiques to be sold again, or treasured, or discarded. The homes themselves have been sold off or handed down. Some of them abandoned until the green work of the earth finally brought them down into a conversation of elements.

And yet. The birds still sing with their throats made of autumn, or with a clarity the spring assumes after a morning rain – just as the birds once sang for you, Francis. They sing from the hedges, from the rooftops, or as they fly over the green contours of the Irish countryside, over the land that never failed your pen or left your heart.

I have sat beneath the shady willow to read your poems, travelling a century back in time. And Francis, I'm filled with questions. I cannot fathom Gallipoli. Or that you could write poems afterward. I was an infantryman in Iraq from 2003-2004, but I don't dare to imagine, not even for a second, that I have the slightest clue about the sheer amount of carnage and suffering and pain and terror and unrelenting horror you must have witnessed. I've heard more than enough of mortars coming down, the sound of a god cracking the air open, the hammer of a god pounding the ground beneath us, and feared hearing my own name shuddering from the core of those detonations. And I've felt adrenaline fire its wiry animal electricity through the channels of my body. I know a small measure, perhaps, a very small measure, of what your eyes must have taken in. Glimpses, maybe. Fractions.

And still I circle back to the *how* of it … How is it possible that birds continued to sing in your verses? That the 'brown/ nude beauty of the Autumn sweetly bent/ over the woods' and 'with distance, like a little sparking star/ drowned in the lavender of evening sea', and these 'with birds in flight and flowers in bloom'? I look at my own journal from my time in a combat zone, and I find rare moments of that backwards glance, that look over the shoulder – the way your eyes looked back across the water to find a vision of home. But I think I have it all wrong. Ireland exists within. For you, Francis, the blackbirds never stopped singing. The bowers continued to offer their refuge beneath them. And the old footpaths remained in their bucolic state as an invitation for you to walk into the fields of the world. And so, if there is a heaven, or a version of it, it grew within, and it was this place you visited when sunk in the mud, shells hunting in the night sky above.

In a sense, you were already a ghost, and your poems offer us the voice of one who haunts a deeply loved world. Your poems were recitals for all that would follow after the last shell found its mark, killing you and four other men as you drank tea in a pit of mud. And the men who fired that round, would they have reversed the course of that ordnance if only once they heard a poem about how sad and lonely the war made you, if they could have read a few lines, maybe, to get a small sense of the mind that thought this:

> *And when the war is over I shall take*
> *My lute a-down to it and sing again*
> *Songs of the whispering things amongst the brake,*
> *And those I love shall know them by their strain.*
> *Their airs shall be the blackbird's twilight song,*
> *Their words shall be all flowers with fresh dews hoar.*
> *But it is lonely now in winter long,*
> *And, God! to hear the blackbird sing once more.*

from 'The Place'

Francis, when people speak of you and your work, they so often seem to focus on your place in a ranking of greatness and accomplishment. They wrangle over the quality of your lines, as even Lord Dunsany himself seems to have done, though he was among your greatest champions. I am not eager to join in their ranks, to weigh the measures and place a judgment on their merit for inclusion or exclusion from the literary canon. How could I? We don't even have all of your poems to consider. I served with the 10th Mountain Division as a NATO soldier in northern Bosnia, garrisoned just off the Sava river, with a hard winter of freezing ice and blizzards of snow, and I think of that harsh winter you spent in the mountains of Serbia, in far more difficult and deadly conditions than I faced, and how you lost many of your poems there, poems that must have brought, when the following spring came, green shades of County Meath to the hillsides and the valleys, a verdant wonder to any who might have passed by. And I also wonder what the world would have gained had you never enlisted, or if you could have found a way to desert the uniform after the execution of your friend, the poet Thomas MacDonagh, when the events of the Easter Rising changed everything. You were only 29 when you exhaled that last breath. I was just getting started at 29. I've had two decades more to catch my stride and I'm only now beginning to learn the intricacies of the line. Your rhymes would have deepened and slipped more into the interior of the poems. Your conversations with contemporaries and their work would have heightened your sense of pace and fluidity, your ability to shift and move a poem within the body of form. I'm certain of this, though it does you no good in your cold Belgium grave.

I write this letter to you now, Francis, because I want you to know something. I intend to bring flowers to your grave, there in the Artillery Wood Military Cemetery in Boezinge, Belgium. Plot 2, Row B, Grave 5. And, if I find myself near your beloved Ellie's grave, somewhere near Manchester, I believe, I'll do my best to pay her grave a visit, too. I'll read some of your poems to her, saying – 'Do you remember how each puff of wind/ made every wing a hum? My hand in yours/ was listening to your heart.' And I'll leave flowers there, too, in your name, Francis, saying –

> A blackbird singing
> I hear in my troubled mind,
> Bluebells swinging
> I see in a distant wind.
> But sorrow and silence
> Are the wood's threnody,
> The silence for you
> And the sorrow for me.

I send my best to you, Francis, one poet to another ...

March, 2017

## HERE, BULLET ✹ *Brian Turner*

If a body is what you want,
then here is bone and gristle and flesh.
Here is the clavicle-snapped wish,
the aorta's opened valves, the leap
thought makes at the synaptic gap.
Here is the adrenaline rush you crave,
that inexorable flight, that insane puncture
into heat and blood. And I dare you to finish
what you've started. Because here, Bullet,
here is where I complete the word you bring
hissing through the air, here is where I moan
the barrel's cold oesophagus, triggering
my tongue's explosives for the rifling I have
inside of me, each twist of the round
spun deeper, because here, Bullet,
here is where the world ends, every time.

from *Here, Bullet* (Alice James Books, 2005)

Trysting stone, Janeville

## LEDWIDGE ✖ *Michael Longley*

I can imagine his last sup of tea,
Milky and sweet, elbow on knee, body
Parts, his fingers caressing the mess-tin,
His steamy moustache whispering a girl's name.

TRENCHES.

The Battalion went on a working
party. East side of the Canal worked
on road: STEAM MILL 28/B 6 d 3.3 to
Railway 28/C 1 C 7.3. Left FOREST
CAMP area at 13.30 returning at
22.30. Casualties during work:
2 Lt. W.E. Cuming killed
5 O.R. killed 1 O.R. D.of W. 18 W.
Work was done on ground captured
from the Germans during the morning
zero hour being 3.50 a.m.

                    J. SHERWOOD-KELLY
                          Lieut.Colonel,
        Commanding 1/R. Inniskilling Fusiliers.

Royal Inniskilling Regimental diary, August 1917
*(courtesy of the Francis Ledwidge Museum)*

Roses will bloom in lanes in Meath
for a thousand years to come,
and blackbirds will charm other hearts,
and the Boyne still sweep to the sea,
and others may love these things
as Ledwidge loved them,

                    but they were
all so much pictured upon his heart
and he sang so gladly of them,
that something is lost which those fields
would have given up and may never give again.


**DUNSANY**

excerpt from *Irish Life*, 10 August 1917

# NOTES ON CONTRIBUTORS

RICHARD BALL, with Navan Youth Theatre in 1987, devised *Ledwidge Sings Slane*, a play based on the life and legend of Francis Ledwidge which was performed at the Conyngham Arms, Slane and broadcast by RTÉ on John Quinn's *The Open Mind*. His short story 'The Chamber Pot' was awarded second place in the Francis MacManus Short Story Competition 2013 and performed as a dramatic monologue at Solstice Arts Centre, Navan in November 2015. He is partial to a good walk.

EAVAN BOLAND is Bella Mabury and Eloise Mabury Knapp Professor in Humanities at Stanford University and has published nine volumes of poetry, including *Against Love Poetry, The Lost Land, In a Time of Violence*, and *An Origin Like Water: Collected Poems 1967-87*. She has received the Lannan Award for Poetry and has published a volume of prose titled *Object Lessons: The Life of the Woman and the Poet in Our Time*.

PADRAIC COLUM's (1881-1972) numerous poetry collections include *Wild Earth* (1916), *Dramatic Legends and Other Poems* (1922), *Collected Poems* (1953), and *Irish Elegies* (1958). Colum also edited *An Anthology of Irish Verse* (1948). His folklore-based works include the *Treasury of Irish Folklore* (1954) and *The Stone of Victory and Other Tales* (1966). His biographies include *Our Friend James Joyce* (1958) and *Ourselves Alone!: The Story of Arthur Griffith and the Origin of the Irish Free State* (1959).

GERALD DAWE's eight collections of poetry are published by The Gallery Press including *Selected Poems* (2012) and *Mickey Finn's Air* (2014). He edited *Earth Voices Whispering: an anthology of Irish war poetry 1914-1945* (Blackstaff, 2008) and has published *Of War and War's Alarms: Reflections on Modern Irish Writing* (Cork University Press, 2015) which contains a chapter on Francis Ledwidge. He is Professor Emeritus and Fellow of Trinity College Dublin.

SEÁN DUNNE (1956-1995) published three collections, *Against the Storm* (Dolmen, 1985) and – with The Gallery Press – *The Sheltered Nest* (1992) and *Time and the Island* (1996). He edited *Poets of Munster*, *The Cork Anthology*, and *Something Understood*. His *Collected* was published in 2005 and reprinted in 2015.

PETER FALLON continues to direct The Gallery Press which he founded in February 1970. His recent books include *The Georgics of Virgil* (Oxford World Classics) and *Strong, My Love*. *Deeds and Their Days (after Hesiod)* is forthcoming. A member of Aosdána and honorary member of the RHA, he lives in Loughcrew in County Meath.

TOM FRENCH's collections, the most recent being *The Way to Work* (2016), are published by The Gallery Press. In 2010, with Frances Tallon, he edited *A Meath Anthology* (Meath County Council Library Service). He lives with his family close to where Ledwidge 'courted at the seaside/ Beyond Drogheda'.

CON HOULIHAN's (1925-2012) publications include *More Than a Game*, *A Harvest: New, Rare and Uncollected Essays*, *Close the Wicket Gate: Tales from the Kilmichael Bar*, *Death of a King and Other Stories*, *In So Many Words: The Best of Con Houlihan*, and *Windfalls*.

MICHAEL LONGLEY's ten collections have received many awards, among them the Whitbread Prize, the TS Eliot Prize, the Hawthornden Prize, and the Griffin International Prize. He was appointed a CBE in 2010 and was Ireland Professor of Poetry from 2007 to 2010. In 2015 he was elected a Freeman of the City of Belfast where he and his wife, the critic Edna Longley, live and work. His most recent collection is *Angel Hill* (Jonathan Cape, 2017).

JOHN McAULIFFE is an Irish poet who has lived and worked in England since 2002. His fourth book, joint winner of the 2016 Michael Hartnett Prize, is *The Way In* (The Gallery Press). His anthology *Everything to Play For: 99 Poems About Sport* (Poetry Ireland) was longlisted for the 2016 Eir Sports Book of the Year. The Gallery Press also publish his *Of All Places* (2011), which was a PBS Recommendation, *Next Door* (2007) and *A Better Life* (2002), which was shortlisted for a Forward prize. He co-directs the Centre for New Writing at the University of Manchester where he teaches poetry and co-edits *The Manchester Review*. He also writes a regular poetry column for *The Irish Times*.

THOMAS MacDONAGH's (1878-1916) works include *Through the Ivory Gate, April and May, When the Dawn is Come, Songs of Myself, Lyrical Poems, Thomas Campion and the Art of English Poetry*, and *Literature in Ireland* (published posthumously).

CATHAL BUÍ MAC GIOLLA GHUNNA (c.1680-1756) was born in County Fermanagh and dedicated some time to reading for the priesthood before settling for the career of rake-poet.

BERNARD O'DONOGHUE was born in Cullen, County Cork in 1945 and still spends part of the year there. Since 1965 he has lived in Oxford where he is now an Emeritus Fellow of Wadham College. He has published seven volumes of poems, of which the most recent is *The Seasons of Cullen Church* (Faber, 2016).

GERARD SMYTH has published nine collections of poetry, including, *The Yellow River*, with artwork by Seán McSweeney (Solstice Arts Centre, 2017), *A Song of Elsewhere* (Dedalus Press, 2015), and *The Fullness of Time: New and Selected Poems* (Dedalus Press, 2010). A sequence of poems, *After Easter*, with a drawing by artist Brian Maguire was published in a limited edition by The Salvage Press in 2016. He was the 2012 recipient of the O'Shaughnessy Poetry Award and is co-editor of *If Ever You Go: A Map of Dublin in Poetry and Song* (Dedalus Press) which was Dublin's One City One Book in 2013. He is a member of Aosdána and Poetry Editor of *The Irish Times*.

JESSICA TRAYNOR's debut collection *Liffey Swim* (Dedalus Press, 2014) was nominated for the 2015 Strong/Shine Award. Awards include the Ireland Chair of Poetry bursary 2014, Hennessy New Irish Writer 2013, and the Listowel Poetry Prize 2011. In 2016 the Arts Council and Irish Writers Centre commissioned a 1916 centenary poem, and a verse response to Swift's *A Modest Proposal* is forthcoming in 2017 from The Salvage Press.

BRIAN TURNER is the author of a memoir, *My Life as a Foreign Country* and two collections of poetry: *Here, Bullet* and *Phantom Noise*. He also co-edited *The Strangest of Theatres: Poets Writing Across Borders*. Turner served for seven years in the US Army. He was an infantry team leader for a year in Iraq (2003-2004) and he deployed to Bosnia-Herzegovina with the 10th Mountain Division (1999-2000). His poetry and essays have been published in *The New York Times, National Geographic, Poetry Daily, The Georgia Review, Virginia Quarterly Review* and other journals. He is the founding director of the MFA program at Sierra Nevada College in Lake Tahoe.

KATHARINE TYNAN (1859-1931) wrote more than 100 novels, 12 collections of short stories, reminiscences, plays, and more than a dozen books of poetry, among them *Louise de la Vallière and Other Poems* (1885), *Shamrocks* (1887), *Ballads and Lyrics* (1891), *Irish Poems* (1913), *The Flower of Peace: A Collection of the Devotional Poetry of Katharine Tynan* (1914), *Flower of Youth: Poems in Wartime* (1915), and *Late Songs* (1917). Her two sons fought in the First World War.

DAVID WHEATLEY is the author of various books of poetry and prose, including *The President of Planet Earth* (Carcanet, 2017). He edited the *Poems* of James Clarence Mangan for Gallery Press (2003) and Samuel Beckett's *Selected Poems 1930-1989* for Faber and Faber (2009). His *Reader's Guide to Essential Criticism of Contemporary British Poetry* was published by Palgrave in 2014. He lives in rural Aberdeenshire.

GARETH YORE, a native of Slane, is the third generation of his family to be engaged in the work of keeping the memory of Francis Ledwidge alive.

# ACKNOWLEDGEMENTS

Warm thanks are due to the following individuals, publishers and institutions who contributed generously to this publication:
Gerald Dawe
Eavan Boland
Brian Turner
Michael Longley
John McAuliffe
Bernard O'Donoghue
Jessica Traynor
Peter Fallon
Gerard Smyth
Richard Ball
David Wheatley
The Francis Ledwidge Committee
The Evening Press
The British Library
The National Library of Ireland
Meath County Council Library Service
Meath County Council
Studies: An Irish Quarterly Review
Poetry Ireland / Éigse Éireann
Bloodaxe Books
Faber & Faber
The Gallery Press
The literary estates of Seán Dunne, Padraic Colum, Katharine Tynan, Con Houlihan and Lord Dunsany
Belinda Quirke, Solstice Arts Centre
Ciarán Mangan and Frances Tallon, Meath County Council Library Service
Maureen Kennelly, Paul Lenehan and Sarah Guinan of Poetry Ireland
Niall McCormack
Trish Edelstein
Colm, Gareth & Rosemary Yore